# TRANSVESTISM, TRANSSEXUALISM IN THE PSYCHOANALYTIC DIMENSION

# CONTROVERSIES IN PSYCHOANALYSIS SERIES

# TRANSVESTISM, TRANSSEXUALISM IN THE PSYCHOANALYTIC DIMENSION

*edited by*

*Giovanna Ambrosio*

Controversies in Psychoanalysis Series

**KARNAC**

First published in 2009 by
Karnac Books Ltd
118 Finchley Road, London NW3 5HT

British Library Cataloguing in Publication Data

A C.I.P. for this book is available from the British Library

ISBN 978 1 85575 765 3

Edited, designed and produced by The Studio Publishing Services Ltd
www.publishingservicesuk.co.uk
e-mail: studio@publishingservicesuk.co.uk

Printed in Great Britain

www.karnacbooks.com

# CONTENTS

# IPA Publications Committee

The present Publications Committee of the International Psychoanalytical Association continues with this volume the new series, Controversies in Psychoanalysis, the objective of which is to reflect, within the frame of our publishing policy, present debates and polemics in the psychoanalytic field.

Theoretical and clinical progress in psychoanalysis continues to develop new concepts and to reconsider old ones, often in contradiction with each other. By confronting and opening these debates, we might find points of convergence, but also divergences that cannot be reconciled; the ensuing tension among these should be sustained in a pluralistic dialogue.

The aim of this series is to focus on these complex intersections through various thematic proposals developed by authors from within different theoretical frameworks and from diverse geographical areas, in order to open possibilities of generating a productive debate within the psychoanalytic world and related professional circles.

The present title focuses on transsexualism, a subject that generates deep controversies from different points of view: psychoanalytic, cultural, social, and ethical. Gender identity and sexuality are at play as well as the real possibility of changing sex through surgical procedures. The editor and the contributors have accepted the challenge to consider and display these debates.

We are pleased to continue this series with the support of Cláudio Eizirik, President of the International Psychoanalytical Association. Special thanks are due to the editor, Giovanna Ambrosio, and to the contributors to this volume.

Leticia Glocer Fiorini
Chair of the Publications Committee

**Jacqueline Amati Mehler** is a training and supervising analyst of the Italian Psychoanalytical Association (AIPsi). Born in Europe, she emigrated to Argentina in 1938. She graduated from Medical School at the University of Buenos Aires, and trained in Adult and Child Psychiatry (Harvard Medical School). She then emigrated to Italy in 1964, where she trained as a psychoanalyst. She was Secretary to the IPA during the presidency of Professor J. Sandler (1989–1993), and was involved in many IPA committees, in particular those concerned with training matters. She was elected Vice-President of IPA in 1997. She served on the European Board of the *International Journal of Psychoanalysis,* and founded and is currently the Director of *Psicoanalisi,* the journal of her Association. In 1997, she was the recipient of the Sigourney Award. She has authored several articles, essays and chapters in books, including co-authoring *The Babel of the Unconscious* (1993), first published in Italian, then translated into various languages, and currently the second edition is in press in Germany. She has a full-time psychoanalytic clinical practice in Rome, and her main interest is in early mental processes, memory, and symbolic function development, as well as in the theory and technique of the psychoanalytic treatment of psychoses.

**Giovanna Ambrosio** is a full Member of the Italian Psychoanalytical Association and the IPA, past secretary of the Italian Psychoanalytical Association, and Chief Editor of the journal *Psicoanalisi*. She is the current overall Chair of the IPA Committee on Women and Psychoanalysis (COWAP), and former European co-chair of the Committee on Women and Psychoanalysis (2001–2005). Her main scientific interests include the field of the intrapsychic interaction relationship between "truth and false", the meanings of "lies", and issues related to the well known problem of the "confusion of tongues". She is author of several essays and editor of two books.

**Simona Argentieri** is a full Member of the IPA, and a training and supervising analyst of the Italian Psychoanalytical Association (AIPsi). Her main interests include the mind–body relationship, psychosomatic medicine, and gender identity. She has published extensively in these fields. Besides her full-time clinical practice, she has been involved in the field of bio-ethics, in teaching at universities, and in active psychoanalytic divulgences in the mass media. She has dedicated much thought to the relationship between psychoanalysis and culture and art, particularly the cinema. She is the author of many essays and books on the above subjects.

**Colette Chiland** read philosophy and psychology, then medicine and psychiatry, at the University of Paris. She taught clinical psychology at La Sorbonne, then at University Paris Descartes, and is a training analyst at the Paris Psychoanalytical Society. She was psychiatrist-in-chief at the Alfred-Binet Centre, and is Honorary President of the International Association for Child and Adolescent Psychiatry and Allied Professions. She has authored nine books and about 400 papers on various topics of psychoanalysis (*Homo psychanalyticus*) and child and adolescent psychiatry (school failure, work with schools and family). She has edited many books in French and co-edited in English *Long-term Treatment of Psychotic States*, and nine books of the series "The Child in His Family". During the past three decades, she has dedicated part of her time to the study of gender identity, its construction and vicissitudes. Three of her books on this theme have been translated into English: *Transsexualism: Illusion and Reality* (Sage, 2003); *Exploring Transsexualism* (Karnac, 2005); and *Sex Makes the World Go Round* (Karnac,

2008). Her most recent book (in French) is devoted to reflections on the human condition and the "absolute evil" human beings are able to do to other human beings.

**Domenico Di Ceglie** is a Consultant Child and Adolescent Psychiatrist in the Adolescent Department and Director, Gender Identity Development Service at the Tavistock & Portman NHS Trust, and Honorary Senior Lecturer, The Royal Free and University College Medical School, London. Previously, he was Visiting Professor in Adolescent Psychiatry, University of Perugia, Italy. He has a long-standing interest in adolescence and has worked in adolescent in-patient units. He has been widely involved in consultative work to organizations and to professional networks. He has been Organizing Tutor of an MA course in Adolescent Mental Health for professionals. In 1989, he founded a specialist unit for children, adolescents, and their families facing gender identity issues at St George's Hospital, London, now based at the Tavistock & Portman NHS Foundation Trust. The unit provides a multi-disciplinary service countrywide, consultation, training, and research. He has developed models of care and treatment for children and adolescents with gender identity disorder. He has published papers about his work and edited a book, *A Stranger in My Own Body: Atypical Gender Identity Development and Mental Health* (Karnac). He was highly commended in the Health & Social Care Awards, 2004. He gives lectures in the UK and abroad.

**Eulàlia Torras de Beà** is a psychiatrist specializing in children and teenagers, training psychoanalyst of the Spanish Psychoanalytical Society, and a children's and teenagers' psychoanalyst. In 1969, she founded a centre for psychiatry and psychology in Barcelona, within the Red Cross Hospital, for children and teenagers, which has since become the Fundació Eulàlia Torras de Beà. Today, more than fifty people work in this Service. She has published the following books: *¿Qué es ser niño?* (Gaya Ciencia, 1977); *Dislexia, pensamiento, aprendizaje* (Pediátrica, 1977); *Entrevista y Diagnóstico en psiquiatría infantil psicoanalítica* (Paidós, 1991); *Grupos de hijos y de padres en psiquiatría infantil psicoanalítica* (Paidós, 1996); and *Dislexia en el desarrollo psíquico* (Paidós, 2002). In July 2007, she published: *Normalidad, psicopatología y tratamiento en niños, adolescentes y familia*

(Lectio). She is the "compiladora", and has published many specialist articles on psychoanalysis.

**Estela V. Welldon** is the Founder and Honorary Elected President
for Life of the International Association for Forensic Psychotherapy.
She is Fellow of the Royal College of Psychiatrists, Honorary Doctor
in Sciences, Oxford Brookes University, and Honorary Consultant
Psychiatrist in Psychotherapy at Tavistock Portman NHS Clinics.
She is a member of the British Association for Psychotherapy, the
Confederation of British Psychotherapists, the Institute of Group
Analysis, the American Group Analysis, and of the International
Association of Group Psychotherapy. She is also an honorary mem-
ber of the Society of Couple Psychoanalytic Psychotherapists,
Tavistock Clinic, and has authored *Mother, Madonna, Whore: The
Idealization and Denigration of Motherhood* (1988); *Sadomasochism*
(2002); and is the main editor of *A Practical Guide to Forensic Psychotherapy* (1997). She has written extensively on the unique contribution of group analytical psychotherapy applied to the forensic
patient. She lectures worldwide, is a member of the teaching staff
at several universities, works privately as a psychoanalytical psychotherapist, is a trained organizational consultant, and a consultant to the media on television, films, and to the arts in general.

# FOREWORD

This book contains some of the papers presented at the European Conference on the theme of transsexualism that, as chair of the IPA Committee on Women and Psychoanalysis (COWAP), I had the privilege to organize in Catania, Italy, on the 17 and 18 April 2006; in particular, the papers of Simona Argentieri, Colette Chiland, Domenico Di Ceglie, Eulàlia Torras de Beà, and Estela Welldon, psychoanalysts and psychotherapists who are especially interested in themes related to gender identity and perversions. To these papers have been added the contribution of Jacqueline Amati Mehler, who co-ordinated the discussion and contributed with the conclusive Counterpoints.

The philosophy of our Committee is to concentrate on questions of strong social impact, with special attention to the theoretical and clinical psychoanalytical quality. It is also our tradition to work around a feminine and masculine image as a "whole", while trying to illuminate—through our psychoanalytic thinking—the "shaded areas".

The theme that we have chosen for our reflections represents quite a challenge, precisely because it is included in these "shaded areas". From a psychoanalytical–theoretical viewpoint, there is obviously an interweaving of different levels to be unravelled, and it is this difficult task that has confronted the psychoanalysts and psychotherapists who have contributed to this book.

I think that the diversity of these contributions is fundamental, but also, at the same time, the minimum of common denominator that unites them: that is, paying attention to the need to link psychoanalytic theory to clinical experience, and always taking into consideration the "experiential" quality of psychoanalytic theory and the study of the psychopathology (Gaddini, 1984). This seems to be the invisible thread that binds these works together, and helps us to look at this thorny and complex theme from different points of view.

## Acknowledgements

I wish to thank all those who have agreed to contribute to this book, thus allowing us to reflect on transsexualism with the hope that it may stimulate and reinforce theoretical and clinical interest in such a crucial "hot" theme.

On behalf of all the Committee on Women and Psychoanalysis, I wish to thank the IPA Publications Committee, and particularly Leticia Glocer Fiorini, who trusted in us and helped us transform a wish into reality.

I also wish to thank the copy-editor of this book, Yvonne Doney.

Last but not least, a special thank to the IPA President, Claudio Eizirik, and also to IPA Secretary Monica Armesto, for their continuing support to our Committee.

## Reference

Gaddini, E. (1984). Changes in psychoanalytic patients up to the present day. In: R. S. Wallerstein (Ed.), Changes in analysts and in their training. *The Int. Psychoanal. Ass. Monograph Series, 4*: 6–19.

Giovanna Ambrosio
Editor

# Introduction[1]

*Giovanna Ambrosio*

"... Sici, ubi complexu coierunt membra tenaci,
nec duo sunt sed forma duplex, nec femina dici
nec puer ut possit, nec ut rumque et utumque videtur ..."

(Ovidio Nasone, Metamorphoseon, IV: 377–379,
Zanichelli, Bologna 1981)

"Thus, the two bodies fused closely together are no longer
two, but from their double aspect it cannot be told whether
they are male or female: one seems to be the other, from their
appearance, although they are neither of the two ..."

## The purpose of the book

The subject chosen as a theme for reflection-transsexualism—is a
many-sided theme[2] that could be considered as a paradigmatic
interpretation of the society in which we live. As stated in the
Foreword, confronting it from the psychoanalytic viewpoint represents quite a challenge, precisely because it is inscribed in the
"shaded areas" of sexuality: an area in which the already complex

concept of identity—in its turn containing others such as incorpora-
tion, imitation, projective identification, adhesive identification,
and introjection—becomes even more complex.

But the theme of transsexualism involves us also on another
plane: with patients such as these, we must focus in a more direct
way than usual not only on the intrapsychical and interpsychical
level, but at the same time we must keep in mind deontological and
social-cultural issues. What is more, we are behind the times compared with the growing amount of medical, political–sociological,
cultural, and mass media attention that is being paid to this theme.

From the theoretical–psychoanalytical viewpoint, this naturally
contains an interweaving of different levels that must be unravelled. This makes it even more necessary and important to assume a
rigorous position from the metapsychological viewpoint, while
guarding ourselves against every kind of ideological conformism
that today, unfortunately, seems to prevail in the cultural, and particularly in the psychological, scenario.

In the psychoanalytic or, more often, as we shall see, in the psy-
chotherapeutical situation with a transsexual patient, everything is
made harder by the "public" nature of this condition whereby the
territory becomes "invaded", as it were, by medical, legal, and
social complexities. Confronting the theme of transsexualism, therefore, means coming to terms with this difficult interweaving.

There are now beginning to be special hospital departments,
medical assistance, and psychological support for sex changes, and
colleagues who work in public institutions report an increase in the
requests for help on the part of transvestites and transsexuals.
Because of this, it is perhaps not only by chance that psychoanalysts
have only a few transsexual patients.

Therefore, the choice of this theme arose not only from the
clinical and theoretic interest in the disorders of sexual identity or
of gender identity (I leave it to the book to clarify these two ways
of defining the problem from the semantic–conceptual aspect), but
it also arose from the need to think about the relative "absence" of
such patients in analytic treatment.

It is for this reason that I am happy to have gathered together
here authors such as Argentieri, Chiland, Di Ceglie, Torras de Beà,
and Welldon, who are among the few to represent, at the international level, a reference point in clinical experience relative to this

theme both in the psychoanalytic and the psychotherapeutic field. To Jacqueline Amati Mehler, through her effective conclusive Counterpoints, falls the task of summing up from the psychoanalytic conceptual and clinical–theoretical viewpoint.

## The psychoanalytic neutrality: the difference between rigour and rigidity

I think that a reply to the question about the "absence" that I mentioned above is a complex one, and involves a reflection on our whole discipline: from the issue of the analysability of early levels of psychic organization to that of the fundamental paradigm of asymmetry in the couple at work; from the importance of the setting to the risk of ambiguity and compliance; and to the growing and obsequious cliché (unfortunately, also sometimes used for marketing purposes) about the presumed severe rigidity of psychoanalysis, in which what is lost is the basic difference between rigour and rigidity.

But, above all, it would seem to be an "absence" that is not casual, in as much as the transgender patient (and once again I leave it to the authors to clarify the semantic–conceptual terminology) confronts us more violently than other patients with a scenario in which the fantasy—often in the phase of realization—of manipulating one's own body is the protagonist of the scene.

Could not the analytic situation, therefore, risk becoming a scenario that is too difficult and painful; a place where it is often the case of walking a tightrope in order to distinguish the physiological capacity to have illusions from everything pathological and falsified that can be hidden in it?

This leads us to reflect on the meaning of psychoanalytic neutrality, another fundamental of our discipline. Does being neutral still mean a capacity to listen to all the parts of our patients? Understood as tacit consent, could not neutrality slip dangerously into a compliant attitude, ambiguous and not very protective for a male/female patient?

Clinically, they are situations that confront us with a particular difficulty from the transferential and countertransferential viewpoint. In fact, these clinical situations seem to be characterized, in a "special" way compared with other situations, not only by an uncanny (*Umheimlich*) quality, as might be expected, but by the particular intensity of the anger, pain, and impotence that forge a pathway within ourselves.

It is a little like being consigned all the mortification of a part that has been offended, maltreated, broken into pieces, but, in this case (and this is what makes this intensity so special), all this has already been enacted, or else the process is *in fieri*. Without a symbolic trace, the concrete rawness of these situations—through their de-humanizing reification—generates a particular resonance. We are confronted with bodies that have been enslaved by a dictatorial psychic area. As the reader will observe, particularly in the work of Argentieri, we are confronted with the triumph of sensuality over sexuality, in which the Freudian "drive sacrifice" becomes a concrete thing; it is represented to us by a "de-constructed" corporeity in which, sometimes, it seems that the "new" that has been achieved is more of a loss of shape than a new shape, and, thus, a new sexual identity.

The disarticulation, the detachment, of the body from the mind often emerges through a physiognomy that is very obviously fake, and in which any trace of an authentic spontaneous gesture seems to have been lost. Sometimes, through the retaining of an instinctive gesture (a glance, a tone of voice, a different way of shaping the lips when speaking), pitiful vestiges of a sexual gender that has been betrayed or lost for ever, we seem to see the command of that "Mafia gang" (Rosenfeld, 1971) that has by now imposed its authority. This situation has been very well described by a psychoanalyst who had a difficult case in treatment:[3] "his/her masculine (or feminine) body has been mortified and destructively attacked, but at the same time their behaviour attacks and ridicules the 'new body'". A painful condition, therefore, marked by a quality that is grotesque and destructive at the same time.

In other words, transsexualism is a theme to which we, as psychoanalysts, must restore its own autonomous theoretic and clinical space in order to remove it from the confusion and blackmail of every type of ideological conformism (Argentieri). It is a "risky" theme in which we must navigate between the Scylla of focusing attention only on the functioning of the mind, and the Charybdis of a reality that is only bodily (Di Ceglie).

## The contents of the book

I think that this book will help us to think and reflect clinically, enabling us to work on a theoretical resignification of this crucial theme. In fact, here, the theme of transvestism and transsexuality has certainly gained in consistency from the theoretical as well as the clinical viewpoint.

The protagonists of our discourse are psychoanalysts of adult patients, and psychoanalysts and psychotherapists of children and adolescents; this means that sometimes it is difficult to make comparisons because of the profound psycho-social diversity of the clinical situations.

For my part, in introducing you to a reading of this book, I shall limit myself to pointing out the two focal issues that, in my opinion, emerge from the book: one regards the structural aspect of our theme; the other is concerned with the "what do I do?" of psychoanalysts when they have to deal with those still rare and sporadic cases of transvestism and transsexualism that may come to their attention.

### The structural aspect

To begin with the first point, we all seem to agree on the pathological and diversified nature of transvestism and transsexualism, with the exception of passing or mixed forms of the same. As far as the structure is concerned, the authors point to the need to distinguish transvestism from transsexualism, even though they would both belong to the area of the perversions.

However, while transvestism corresponds to a more developed stage of the processes of separation–individuation, the Winnicottian transitional area, transsexualism (Argentieri: it is "a typical circumscribed delusion . . .. insensible to the play of illusion") binds the thought process to the concreteness of the body, thus signalling the absence of symbolic thought. According to Chiland, it is also defined as "a narcissistic malady", in as much as transsexuals have great difficulty in constructing a "sense of continuity and of the emergence of their own selves". On the one hand, Argentieri, as will be extensively discussed in final chapter, Counterpoints (Amati Mehler), thinks that it could be seen as a desperate and extreme mutilating solution that, through the body, sacrifices sexuality in favour of a pre-genital "imitative" sensuality, whereas on the other hand, according to Chiland, it might not always be considered as an actual renunciation of sexuality.

Concerning children and the possibility of them developing an atypical form of gender identity, Di Ceglie again proposes his concept of atypical organization of gender identity (AGIO), a clinical entity analysable according to a series of parameters. Emphasis has been put on the need not to stop at the phenomenological aspect of the symptoms, or be content with a mere casual connection, but to explore the internal world of the child and his unconscious fantasies (Torras de Beà) in order to accede to the vicissitudes of the identification processes, and to be able to distinguish "beliefs" from "imagination" (Britton, 1998) or from conscious and unconscious fantasies (Di Ceglie). It seems clear that so-called childhood cross-dressing is not necessarily the prelude to transvestism in adolescence or adulthood.

Consistent with my role as chair of the IPA Committee on Women and Psychoanalysis, I should like to emphasize what I consider to be an interesting "difference" regarding the "feminine dimension", an issue on which there appear to be two different positions.

The first (Argentieri) suggests that we look at transsexualism as the paradigmatic denial of the old assumption that women are exempt from the pathology of perversions. Based on her own clinical experience, she believes that the psychopathological organization of transsexualism is substantially the same in men as in women, and is manifested in "the delusional conviction of belonging to the opposite sex".

The second position (Chiland) is directly and explicitly opposed to the first, and maintains that, as far as the psychopathological structure of the mind is concerned, a rejection of masculinity is not the same thing as a rejection of femininity. In fact, from Chiland's point of view, the rejection of masculinity is the rejection of an activity that is inevitably connected with aggressiveness, while the rejection of femininity is the rejection of passivity.

These two arguments are interesting in as much as they appear to point to two different positions regarding the feminine dimension: one based on a feminine image that is as instinctual, libidinal, aggressive, active/passive as the masculine image; the other anchored to the Freudian passive and non-instinctual image of the women.

## What do we do?

To come now to the second point: what kind of help can the psycho-analyst give to patients who are seeking comprehension and some-times complicity in order to "act out" a transformation of their bodies. It implies again dealing with the meaning of analytic neutrality. As we know, technique (and in our case we must remem-ber that this also includes ethics) goes hand-in-hand with clinical work and with theory, and we all have our own implicit theories (Sandler, & Sandler, 1983) that are stated in our everyday clinical work and in the transference–countertransference interplay.

I believe that neutrality is, in any case, still to be understood as an instrument that allows us to unveil, enter into contact with, and give voice to all the parts of our patient. It is a kind of basic pre-condition to being able to do this work. If it should be lacking, then we are not able to permit our patients access to the symbolization process, and the therapeutic aspect of the analysis is lost. Naturally, this implies paying attention to the type of defences of our patients, but also to our own, and to the risk that the analyst may collude with the patients' more adhesive and harmful defences, first among them that of disavowal.

Regarding this point, I think it is important that there is a sub-stantial basic agreement among our authors on the need to remain neutral. Di Ceglie warns us against the risk of becoming "crusa-ders" in one way or the other; Argentieri invites us to guard against the "two opposite extremes of the sexophobic/sexophilic current—all monsters/all normal—that are collusive allies in discouraging the already slim possibility" that this type of patient would seek real help and real treatment.

Within this basic agreement, however, different and important views are expressed, and I should like to underline Argentieri's particular clinical preoccupation regarding a situation that would suggest a subtle form of collusion on the part of these patients themselves, who "put all their energies at the service of their pro-ject" and who, certain that they can confine their discomfort to the body, search for and find treatment only at the anatomical level. Naturally, a health organization that is little prepared to handle the complex psychic metabolism that these unfortunate situations present, often becomes an accomplice.

I also think it is very important to ask ourselves whether the help that we can give to these patients, when directed towards "re-assignment", can do nothing except sustain a narcissistic–omnipotent–destructive area. We should also ask ourselves to what extent the dramatic moment, when it arrives, of "mentalizing" the irreversibility of the expensive and painful choice that has been made, can activate a breakdown.

This book leaves a significant trace that is both unsaturated as well as provocative: not by chance two characteristics that are typical of the "burning" theme of our discussions.

## Notes

1.  Translated by Jill Whitelaw-Cucco.
2.  There have been many contributions on the theme by philosophers and scholars of bioethics. I mention, in particular, the work of M. Toraldo di Francia, "Lo sconvolgimento del confine". I think it would be useful to focus on the following reflection:

    > The post-modern image of a plastic identity, that confounds all given boundaries—an identity that refuses to incarnate any specific subjectivity, fluid, in perpetual movement, always different, 'without gender connotations, without history and without collocation' (Bordo, 1993, tr. It. p.172)—is not only an anticipatory provocation of new freedoms, a 'critical-innovative' and liberating image compared with the subjugation to old identity constraints and ascribed allegencies. Upon closer inspection, it reveals itself to be more functional to the needs of the new post-industrial capitalism than would appear; from an imaginary viewpoint, it can be seen as the equivalent of the imperatives of a global electronic economy that imposes increasingly malleable and flexible forms of behaviour, faster and faster rhythms of change, and makes the very possibility of personal success depend on the capacity of single individuals to adapt themselves to and accept a prospective of continual change; or, better still, to adopt the new 'ethos' of perpetual mobility. [p. 3]

3.  I refer to a private communication of our colleague Geni Valle.

## References

Britton, R. (1998). *Belief and Imagination—Explorations in Psychoanalysis.* London, New York: Routledge.

Rosenfeld, H. (1971). A clinical approach to the psycho-analytical theory of the life and death instincts: an investigation into the aggressive aspects of narcissism. *International Journal of Psychoanalysis, 52:* 169–178.

Sandler, J., & Sandler, A. M. (1983). The second censorship, the three box model and some technical implication. *International Journal of Psychoanalysis, 64:* 33–45.

Toraldo di Francia, M. (2006). Lo sconvolgimento del confine (unpublished).

# CHAPTER ONE

# Transvestism, transsexualism, transgender: identification and imitation[1]

*Simona Argentieri*

## Retrieval of a psychoanalytic vertex

During the course of a few decades, there has been a dramatic change, both psychologically and in civil rights, in the convulsive social and cultural arena in which transvestites, transsexuals, or the so-called transgendered, live, define themselves, and are defined. Although it is a numerically limited phenomenon, the attention of the media and the consequent involvement of public opinion have been high profile, even though concentrated on certain exceptional cases to which the press has given particular emphasis; for example, two elderly ladies who, thanks to the new British legislation on gay weddings, decided to get married. The bizarre fact was that they had already been married before when one of the couple was a man, before he decided to change sex. Then there was the recent tale of Mrs Sarah Jones, born Colin Jones, who, after a surgical operation, and with the blessings of the ecclesiastical authorities, has become an Anglican pastor.

But apart from these extreme situations, there has certainly been a huge increase in the cases of "trans" both on the stage and on the street, as well as a growing number of more discreet requests for "reassignment of sexual gender" in the specialized centres (more than fifty per month in a public health structure in Northern Italy alone) that would seem to indicate a wish for integration and "normality". It remains to be seen whether there really is an increase in this pathology or whether it has merely come out into the open. Or whether—as I am inclined to think—it is the psychosocial circumstances that favour this type of defence organization.

The problem is that, between scandals and civil disputes, the wish to understand becomes progressively weaker. There are many opinions and not much thought, while the battle continues (mainly in the media), in the form of slogans and proclamations, between the repressive invocations of the conventional thinkers and the demands of the "trans" associations and groups for legal and civil rights.

I think, therefore, that psychoanalysis must laboriously regain an autonomous theoretic and clinical space of its own away from the confusion and blackmail of ideologies.

## Some history

From the psychoanalytic viewpoint, disorders of sexual gender identity at first bore the imprint of the psychiatric nosography of the beginning of the twentieth century, according to a criterion that was prevalently descriptive and phenomenological. A clear distinction was made between *transvestism* (men who had a compulsive urge to dress in women's clothes but who wanted to preserve their psychophysical masculinity) and *transsexualism* (men who hated their own anatomy and desperately wanted to change it into that of a female, whatever the cost). Both syndromes were in any case firmly placed in the category of *perversions*.

As we know, the great Freudian revolution changed the scientific and cultural statute of the perversions; from being the "hereditary taint", "crime", or "sin" of the pre-psychoanalytic age, perversions were traced back to the fountainhead of infancy and of everyday life, even though they were the pathological outcome of drive conflicts in the confrontation with the Oedipal crossroads. There followed the well-known (and then much discussed) axioms of the child as "little perverse polymorph", of perversion as the "negative" of neurosis, of the absence (or almost) of perversions in the female sex, etc.

The various perversions—always listed on a behavioural base, according to the known catalogue of horrors and miseries—were therefore to be defined as fragments of pregenital sexuality, partial undeveloped and unrepressed drives that, deformed by defence mechanisms, take over the leadership of adult sexual organization.

Psychoanalysis, therefore, traces the psychosexual structure back to the developmental history of each individual, and reduces almost to zero (as confirmed by the experiences of R. J. Stoller) those biological factors that had been so emphasized in the past and that, today, have inauspiciously been revived both by those who invoke the laws of nature as well as by those who want to correct a mistake of nature.

Nowadays, however, the language above all has changed, a phenomenon that is never banal when referring to the slippery ground of sexuality. We speak of "gender dysphoria" or "sexual identity disorders"; we use the all-inclusive term of "transgender" that moves the accent from the sexual drive on to gender identity and which, in colloquial terms, has become "trans". Since 1980, in the *DSM-III*, even the term "perversion" has been replaced by the politically correct but ambiguous "paraphilia".

The first question we must ask ourselves, therefore, is whether transvestism and transsexualism can be considered together as one syndrome. The second question is whether it is right to place them among the perversions. This inevitably depends on how we theorize the concept of perversion. In post-Freudian times the term has, in fact, acquired different and progressively extended, diluted, and diversified meanings. The literature on the subject is infinite, although it is not always easy to understand how much the new authors owe to Freud's primary statements. As far as the pathologies are concerned, there is a disparity of views: some place transsexuality among the psychoses (Socarides, 1970), others consider it a precursor of transvestism or homosexuality (Limentani, 1979), a narcissistic disorder (Oppenheimer, 1991; Chiland, 2000) or a borderline disorder (Green, 1986); others, following Lacan, distinguish between psychotic transsexuality and neurotic or perverse forms of transsexualism.

## Clinical work today

The clinical material relevant to transvestites and transsexuals is, of necessity, composite and fragmentary. Personally, I have drawn information from psychoanalytic as well as psychotherapeutic experiences, and also from consultations and supervisions. Inevitably, there are few cases of classic psychoanalysis; as we know, these are patients who are unlikely to seek help from our instruments, both because their symptom is egosyntonic and also because they are dominated by the concreteness of the "acting out" in the body and on the body. More often, and unfortunately, our therapy takes place when the damage has already been done following the failure of other strategies (Quinodoz, 1998). This is confirmed by consultations in specialized centres which provide information that, although it is valuable, concerns patients who are already self-selected and who only rarely commit themselves to a classical analysis. On the other hand, I am very sceptical about the clinical work in the centres that carry out sex "changes", where the patients know that they must convince the psychologist of their authentic motivation. Moreover, the precarious conditions of our public health services usually offer only group therapy or occasional individual interviews of a cognitive type that are of little significance to us.

However, I find that indirect clinical material is useful, such as "occasional findings" during the course of psychoanalysis or psychotherapy undertaken for other reasons.

I take as an example a married man with four children whom he loves dearly. The sexual relationship with his wife is tepid but affectionate. In compensation, he enthusiastically takes part in secret and promiscuous orgies with men. With complete lack of conflict, he greatly enjoys dressing up as a woman at carnival time, or in amateur theatricals, where he acts female parts. He is a successful fashion designer who voluptuously models silks and velvets on himself.

Sometimes, it is the partners of transvestites or transsexuals who ask for a consultation.

A well-dressed and intelligent woman comes to me for treatment. Since childhood she has had a relationship with a pleasant intellectual who makes love—with her consent—dressed and made-up like a woman and calling himself with a woman's name, but only when they make love. In their own way they have a happy relationship and they would like to have a baby.

The baby is born and the couple separates. She continues her analysis while he withdraws in solitude to meditate whether or not to "come out" about his transvestism to his ten-year-old daughter.

It is important to try to understand analytically the relational dynamics of those who accompany, love, or sometimes sexually exploit transvestites and transsexuals in the "grey zone" on the boundary of so-called normality.

I am thinking of an impeccable, highly-placed civil servant who has come to analysis because of troublesome obsessive symptoms, and who occasionally goes in search of transvestite street prostitutes; he greatly enjoys being penetrated by them and feels no conscious conflict.

We must also remember that the peculiarity of the psychoanalytic approach is that it is more interested in the *fantasies* that accompany sexuality than in the manifest behaviour. Nowadays, there are frequent cases of parents who are alarmed by the phenomenon of so-called *infantile cross-dressing*, manifested perhaps in the second year of life. They worry that the infantile transvestism will persist, or that it is the prelude to future homosexuality, while psychoanalysis teaches us that there is no direct correspondence between infantile symptoms and adult pathologies.

Oscar, a little boy of five, with a twin sister, does up his hair with his sister's ribbons and hair-bands and insists on going to open the door to his father, who reacts with anxiety and anger.

## The case of Letizia/Leo

Leo telephones me at the insistence of his doctor who is exasperated by Leo's insatiable requests for steroids and diets to increase his muscle mass that is always less than he would like it to be in spite of tough and exhausting sessions in the gym every day. For Leo was born twenty-seven years ago as Letizia, a name that seems like a mockery in view of his constant unhappiness.

He comes for a consultation with me: a very small young man, with a simple, clean-looking face, a nice smile and a slight beard.

He is dressed simply, in jeans and a black T-shirt that shows off his biceps; his gestures and posture are spontaneously masculine, and it comes naturally to me to address him as a male. I perceive his need for dignity and respect.

> He begins by saying that he doesn't really know why he has come to me, but he feels that "there is something not right". He tells me that he has always felt alone and misunderstood, but the real tragedy was when he began to menstruate and was forced to admit that he was a girl. From that moment on, he was determined to change sex, which he finally managed to do three years ago, with great sacrifices, in a public health structure. Unfortunately, there have been endless medical–surgical complications that have caused him unspeakable physical suffering, disillusion, and deep anger.
>
> I do not ask him anything about the technical aspects of his operations, for fear of seeming to be invasive and voyeuristic, and I think that this enables me to focus his attention on other aspects of his history.
>
> Gradually, I have the impression of a sensitive, intelligent person, slightly melancholy; in other words, an average neurotic who can benefit from psychoanalysis, except for the nucleus regarding his gender identity that he resists with a rock-hard will. Once, when speaking about his past, I addressed him using a feminine pronoun; he completely froze: "This is not under discussion", his look seemed to say.
>
> Later on, he tells me that for a long time he has not had love or sexual relationships; he even avoided masturbation because he felt disgusted by his genitals. When he was a teenager he fell in love with a girl who, however, was not interested in him. At the moment, he has a deep relationship with a professional man who is ten years older than himself. More precisely, he, too, is a transsexual: a woman who has become a man. He had been introduced to him by the psychologist of the public health structure (!) with whom he had a long period of group therapy before and after the "re-assignation".
>
> I point out to him that while, for him, anatomical sex is extremely important, it seems that the sex of the person he loves does not carry the same weight.. "Yes, it was easy! I never thought about it", he says, struck by my remark. I also think, but I do not tell him, that they have constructed a partnership that is fairly solid, but based on mutual help and affection rather than on sexuality and love.

He then tells me that his mother, devoted and distressed, cared for him while he was in hospital although she was very much against the operation, and this finally brought about a slight reconciliation between the two. Only after many months did he explain to me that he had had breasts, uterus, and ovaries removed, but he had not wanted to have plastic surgery on his genitals. "That wasn't important", he said calmly.

He has no plans for further surgery on his genitals that would suit them to his new identity; and I do not think that this is only due to his disillusionment over the mess made by his surgeons. However, he continues to be obsessed by the inadequacy of his muscle mass and his lack of facial hair, the so-called secondary sexual characteristics that should transmit a bodily image of his masculine self that is credible and recognizable as such to other people in his everyday life.

In fact, in Leo's life, there has been very little space for sexuality as pleasure, either through masturbation or as an encounter with another person. At the conscious level he has desperately pursued his project of becoming a man, or, rather, of having a masculine body corresponding to his life events; but, at the unconscious level, he has had to destroy and eliminate his feminine part which was equivalent to a "bad", intolerable part that could not be integrated. His masculine pseudo-identity, of an imitative type, must serve to keep away the threat of persecutory anxieties. The deep equivalence is between bad part and drives, expressed within the concreteness of the flesh. The real drama is that, as the therapy proceeds, he will inevitably have to come to terms with the impossibility of becoming a real man, and, on the other hand, the irreparability of the destruction that has been perpetrated on his body as a woman, with his own complicity, and particularly the definitive renunciation of having children.

## The case of Claudio/Claudette

Claudio is a big man aged forty-three with the face of a little boy. He has come to consult me from a small town in the south, at the strong insistence of his wife. He owns a small, successful business and they have been married for eight years.

In a childish way, self-accusingly but seeking for my indulgence, he tells me that he has a "nasty habit": in his free time he likes to dress up exactly like a housemaid, from the frilly cap to the shoes. For some time now he has also worn a brassière and knickers under the uniform. Dressed up like this, he enjoys doing all the housework. Every now and then he lets the neighbours see him from the window or balcony as he shakes out the rugs; and this exhibition increases his pleasure. But he never masturbates on these occasions.

His wife has put up with his peculiarities for a long time, but recently she has rebelled because Claudio would like to make love to her dressed up like this. He says that their sexual life has always been reciprocally satisfying.

At my invitation, he then tells me an unhappy family story. His father has "always" been ill with an "atypical depression". "He must have passed it on to me a bit", he says, seeking my confirmation. In reality, I guess that C's father is a psychotic who has not been treated properly and has become chronic. It seems that he has transmitted to his son nothing but anxiety and confusion. When Claudio was still a little boy, he told him that he went with prostitutes and had caught the clap. "That was why he only had one testicle! He showed it to me", he commented, as though this was indisputable proof.

His mother was not affectionate, and also his grandparents, with whom he spent much time, were cold, hard and tyrannical. He was sent to a religious school where the priests were very severe. He tells me that once, when he was little, he had kissed another little boy. I am struck by the fact that a little thing like this, touching and banal, is told to me as though it were blameworthy, and perhaps resignified *après coup* as a "symptom". The only affectionate relationship he had, when he was about eighteen, was with a housemaid who was older than himself and had initiated him to sexuality. "It was a beautiful secret", says C. The woman was very sweet; she lovingly dressed him up in her own work clothes and then they made love.

C tells his story with simplicity and innocence; he wants me to understand how lovely and important the moment of dressing up was for him. He is completely unaware of the grotesque and unintentionally comic aspects of the matter.

During the course of the consultations, C paradoxically seems to gain courage. On Internet he finds a group of "men like himself"; they communicate every evening, and at last he feels understood, justified, recognized as an equal. One evening, he decides to take another step:

he will meet his new friends—or rather, his new girl-friends—*en travestie* in a pizzeria. Obviously, he will have to have a new name: he chooses Claudette.

He tells me this with such delight and happiness that I am moved, and at the same time worried. The meeting is a "success". Showing himself as a woman and being treated as such by his girl-friends and by strangers makes him feel genuinely and unusually happy. He is at pains to explain that sex does not come into all this. He continues to love and desire his wife. He only hopes that she will "keep him like this", perhaps even telling him off and punishing him.

In fact, C does not continue with his analysis. His problem is totally egosyntonic; even his fantasies of punishment probably satisfy the masochistic quotas. The conflict is completely exterior, with a wife who does not accept him and he cannot understand why not. It is she who has forced him to consult me, but essentially he hopes that I will be the one to convince his wife. Sadly, I realize that this good and gentle man, naïve and innocent, is consigned into the hands of his wife like a child; however, he is unable to renounce his dressing up, the only area in which he finds a holding, emotions, and tenderness.

I think that the case of Claudio/Claudette is really a classic of transvestism: he feels masculine, he has a masculine sexuality and cares about his genitals, but he has been forced to take refuge from identification with a sick and damaged father. He has had to resort to a feminine (or, rather, feminine phallic) identification, resignified *a posteriori* by the sensual and emotional mirror relationship with the housemaid. When he consciously "plays" at being a woman, he unconsciously brings on to the scene a confused mother–child couple, and keeps his penis hidden like a secret treasure inside women's clothing. Claudio lacked the physiological experience of primal narcissism and of being seen as beautiful and perfect by a mother, long before his problems of sexual gender definition.

I think that, on the wave of castration anxiety, he had organized the perverse solution based on denial and the consequent unequal splitting of the ego. His transvestism is the harmless pathological solution of the Oedipal complex that evades acknowledging the difference between male and female, and that would imply the painful recognition of not being "the wonderful child" and of remaining alone.

## Metapsychological queries

From these brief clinical notes, I think it is clear that there are similarities between Letizia/Leo and Claudio/Claudette. Both of them express their "right" to be seen and recognized by others according to their own internal image. They are both carriers of the claim/hope of reaching an "impossible" solution. Both show a complex interweaving of identificatory and sexual problems at the Oedipal and pre-Oedipal levels. The differences, however, are even more significant and, to my mind, enable us to make some general considerations on these pathologies.

The strategy of transvestism in its way preserves sexuality and the use of drives, accompanied by intense erotization of the transvested body and, not infrequently, more or less explicit quotas of masochism. Transsexualism, on the other hand, provides only the desperate and extreme solution of sacrificing sexuality together with the part of the body that represents it. As I have observed in the case of Leo, his project is the destruction of his female organs.

One can object, however, that male transsexuals (and sometimes also females) want plastic surgery to "construct" for them a simulacrum of the genitals of the desired sex. However, in my opinion, the question does not change, because also in these cases the first step is the removal of penis and testicles and, with them, the capacity of orgasm. The surviving eros is thus entrusted to pregenital sensuality, "imitative" according to Gaddini, superficially sensorial. The resulting feminine pseudo-identity derives pleasure above all from the fact of pleasing and giving pleasure to men, because this provides a reassuring self image that is loving and loved.

The most important difference is the developmental level at which the pathology is organized. Transvestism, to my mind, corresponds to a more evolved stage of the separation–individuation processes, corresponding to the transition phase and area in the Winnicottian sense. It is not coincidental that the symptom is played out mainly with clothes and textiles (inanimate material, therefore), and uses the strategies of play and shared illusion. There come to mind the interesting works of Greenacre and of Gaddini and of Gaddini De Benedetti regarding the pathology of the transitional object and of the comparison between infantile fetishism and pathological arousing transitional object. The thought process of the transsexual, although limited to the nucleus of gender identity, is, on the contrary, bound to the concreteness of the body; it is sunk in reality and is insensible to the play of illusion. The stubborn obstinacy of searching for a solution at the biological level is the symptom of the lack of access to the symbolic, rooted in a pre-symbolic area of incomplete separation between self and not-self.

My answer to the initial queries, therefore, is that we should continue to make a distinction between transvestism and transsexualism, and that both are to be considered, at least theoretically, as perversions.

In contrast with the grim and violent strategy of anatomical devastation, I sometimes think about the fascination, the seduction, the enchantment, the great harmless pleasure of the "shared illusion" that the ambiguities of male/female identity have always offered us through the world of the theatre, art, and fantasy. Under the spotlights, dressing-up exerts a magic fascination on all of us; the rigid laws of reality are momentarily suspended, but without going crazy; the actor *en travestie* expresses something more, possesses a charm and an appeal over and above that of the real woman.

## Structure

Beginning with his famous work on fetishism, Freud investigates the specific, though not exclusive, psychopathological organization of the perversions motivated by castration anxiety: *denial* of the anatomical reality of the difference between male and female, resulting in the *unequal splitting of the ego*. One part of the ego functions and develops normally, while the other, split off and not integrated, denies a quota of perceptive reality: essentially, that of bodily reality and of the symbolic significance of the two great differences between male and female and between adult and child.

Taking into account the many ambiguous, mixed, and passing forms, I think that we must still recognize as the foundation of the clinical picture of transvestism and transsexualism the defensive mechanism typical of the perversion of denial and the consequent unequal structural splitting of the ego. This would explain, in both transsexuals and transvestites, the paradoxical contrast between the relatively well-functioning part of the ego that is in contact with reality, and the circumscribed delusion relative to sexual gender.

## In the feminine dimension

Transsexualism is an explicit refutation of the old assumption that women are exempt from the pathology of perversions (except for masochism, in which our "excellence" has always been recognized). Besides, as long as society—and psychoanalysis—denied that the female sex possessed instincts, whether aggressive or sexual, it was logical that also the pathological deformations would be denied. (Argentieri, 1991)

In my experience, the psychopathological organization of transexualism is substantially the same in men as in women: the delusional conviction (a typical circumscribed delusion) of belonging to the opposite sex, and the compulsive conviction of wanting to regain it, mask the unconscious fantasy of attacking the "bad", drive-dependent part of the body. This part, experienced as being threatening and persecutory, corresponds at the conscious level to the gender identity conferred on them at birth; for them, however, "masculine" or "feminine" correspond only to a defensive splitting, to a pseudo-distinction between partial aspects of the self and of the other.

As I have said on various occasions in the past, the distinctions between mother and father, male and female, are a long and tortuous process (Argentieri, 1988). In fact, both the boy baby and the girl baby must first learn to establish the boundaries between self and not-self, in a dual dimension; and then to recognize the parents not only as "separate" but also as "different" from each other, "not homologous", in a triadic dimension. We know how this process—never completely concluded—is complicated by dangers, compromises, arrests, and defences. Too often, during the course of development, instead of authentic differentiations there can be organized defensive splittings, pseudo-distinctions of partial aspects of self and other, and more or less stable unnatural recompositions that, at the conscious level, regard mother and father, female and male sex, but at the unconscious level, they respond to defensive operations regarding anxieties and conflicts, even at the expense of distorting knowledge.

Thus, for example, the sexual and aggressive drive aspects can be split off and projected on to the father and then on to all males, while the loving, fusional aspects of the relationship remain defensively on the mother. Or vice versa. The splittings can be organized either according to the "classical" horizontal line between "good" and "bad" (penis or breast, alternatively); but also on vertical, primitive or more developed levels of psychism and relationship: Oedipal and pre-Oedipal, loving and erotized, emotional and intellectual, etc. Such unnatural and tortuous splittings often persist into adult age and are organized as "theories" on the male or female nature.

Evidently, the combinations vary considerably, not only according to the basic fact of being born a boy or a girl, but also according to very early relational vicissitudes and the actual characteristics of the parents. The problem, therefore, is on the one hand to discriminate, and on the other hand to integrate, within the self and in relationships, various levels of development and of the area of psychic functioning; that is, to be able to differentiate without splitting, a process that has failed in the case of transexualism.

Again, in my experience, I do not think I have ever come across any real cases of transvestism in females, either adults or children. Certainly, there are women who like to dress in a masculine style, but this is part of a secondary or strategic element, aimed at achieving a concrete and real goal. I have never known women who needed to cross-dress in order to make love, or little girls with the obsession of dressing like boys, or who compulsively drew idealized male figures.

Yet, in the case of a little boy of four years old, so I was told during a supervision, he not only loves dressing in his mother's clothes but is fascinated by the pictures of brides and princesses in magazines. With considerable ability and a wealth of details and colours, he repeatedly draws pictures of princesses with crowns and beautiful long sparkling dresses. He always sleeps with his mother because "he doesn't want to be on his own", say his parents. As a "remedy", they have thrown away his dolls and toy jewellery, telling him that they have been stolen by burglars. As the therapist rightly said: here we need to add something, not take it away!

At the moment I have no answers. Probably, we must continue searching for an explanation for the unequal distribution of transvestism between the sexes through the various solutions relative to castration anxiety.


## Transformation of the concept of perversion

Can we today continue to speak of perversions in general as a single psychopathological group to which corresponds the specific—though not exclusive—structure that Freud singled out in fetishism: the classical defensive combination of denial and consequent splitting of the ego, that saves/safeguards(?) a quota of the personality from psychosis? Or must we sanction its passage from syndrome to generic symptom, and thus be obliged to identify, case by case, the various qualitative and quantitative connotations? In modern psychoanalysis, we see a more or less explicit transformation of the concept that assumes, for different authors, the most subjective and divergent meanings. To give an example at random, Limentani (1977) believes that perversions are by now only "symptoms", for the most part fairly generic and without any specific structure; he thinks that at this present time it is not the psychoanalytic concept of perversion that has changed, but the clinical panorama. However, Bion (1957) and Khan (1979), although using very different theoretical constructions, identify as perverse a particular mental functioning to which corresponds a particular modality of object relation, relatively independent from sexual choices.

Many authors, although they do not mention a specific theoretic model, speak of "perverse transference" derived from a special distorted mode of relations and affects. Chasseguet-Smirgel and McDougall, who operate with radically opposed theoretic conceptualizations, both use the concept of perversion in a very wide scope, ranging from single clinical situations to the socio-political dimension of great historic events such as totalitarianism and wars (see Whitebook, 1991). Other authors speak of perversion as a characterological pathology or as a borderline type of organization.

A significant consequence of disconnecting the perversion concept from the drive concept has been to open the door to feminine perversions (Cooper, 1991). Molfino (1995) suggests the interesting hypothesis that, today, women resort less to maternity as a defence against castration anxiety, and instead, in their "mimetic" desire, use the masculine mechanism of perversion as defence against castration anxiety. Kaplan (1991) moves the objective of sexuality to gender identity and traces another range of unhealthy, perverse behaviour in women, such as kleptomania, self-mutilation, anorexia, etc. Thus, she reinterprets the problem; to the list of classic male perversions, she contrasts the female perversion of variations of gender identity in relation to the socio-cultural context, thus increasingly losing sight of the primitive link not only with the relative structure, but also with the sexual drive.

The most interesting observations on this matter remain those of Welldon, who believes that there have always been feminine perversions, but we just have not wanted to see them. I, too, believe that the positive socio-cultural transformations that have allowed recent generations of women a normal and less inhibited psychosexual development have inevitably had an effect on pathologies, producing clinical situations hitherto unknown. We are beginning to hear of cases of fetishism in women, or of certain patients who, following the classical nineteenth century stereotype of the exhibitionist, suddenly throw open their coats and expose their bare breasts to strangers.

On the other hand, I do not think there is any point in extending the term of "perversion" to cover those many occasional phenomenological situations, together with all the colloquial, allusive meanings that it has acquired recently and that reduce it to a word that is strongly suggestive but extremely vague conceptually. Instead of an enrichment, the result has been a impoverishment in its meaning and a decrease in operative potentiality.

### Very early levels

The concept of gender identity refers to the archaic stages of life when the sense of belonging to the male or female sex begins to be organized within the sphere of relations with the parents, at preverbal and sensorial levels. These developmental events form part of the wider theme of *very early levels* of development that, as we know, represent the most significant broadening of horizons since Freud. Since the 1940s, in fact, psychoanalysis has paid a great deal of attention to the so-called pre-Oedipal, narcissistic levels and to the pathologies that derive from them.

The way in which the question is formulated and confronted depends inevitably on how various authors conceptualize the very early levels. For example, Winnicott postulates a very early phase of existence that is not only pre-Oedipal but also pre-conflictual, in which the drives do not come into play. This is radically opposed to the Kleinian model that sees the drives in action right from the time of birth. Similarly, there are different ways of conceptualizing anxiety at the very early levels: as catastrophic anxieties of annihilation (Winnicott), of integration/non-integration (Gaddini), of persecution (Klein). Consequently, there are different ways for trying to explain transsexualism and transvestism (or transgender, as long as the meaning is specified), by giving greater or less importance to drive vicissitudes and to what happens before or what happens after.

## Aggressiveness and narcissism

We all agree that at the root of these pathologies there is a narcissistic damage, a self-image that is inadequate and underrated, that attempts maniacal reparation. Transsexualism, writes Chiland (2003), is "a malady of narcissism". The fantasies that accompany transvestism, or even more so the change of sex, are experienced as being the carriers of security and well-being, of a consolidation of the "sense of self" that Winnicott speaks about. But, as Oppenheimer (1991) comments, in the transsexual there is also an unconscious hatred of the two parents who have been deprived of their principal generative function. The "new birth" celebrates this maniacal triumph and guarantees "narcissistic benefits".

When comparing today's psychopathology with that of the past, I think we must take into account the role that aggressiveness, together with libido, has assumed, regardless of the theoretical statute entrusted to it by the various authors from Freud onwards. By now we all know that it is not Eros that motivates the pervert, but desperation and anger at the inexorable failure of the gratification experiences that condemns him to compulsive and endless repetition. In transvestites, and also in transsexuals, it is not the libido that motivates the perverse solution, but the impelling need to exorcise the anxiety relative to destructiveness in the relationship. The fantasy of maniacal reparation by constructing the anatomy of the opposite sex is, I think, secondary. The doctor and the surgeon must be the ones to execute it, and the psychologist is the compliant witness.

In the identification–disidentification play, each individual gradually constitutes his or her own gender identity and that of the other, more as a dynamic network of relationships than as a rigid structure. In my opinion, the male or female identity of each person is the result of the more or less happy and harmonious integration of various levels: (1) a first *anatomical, biological* level (with a specific genotypical, phenotypical, hormonal, etc., substratum); (2) a second level of *gender* and of the *psychological sense of appurtenance* (according to Stoller, 1968), that must be articulated within the relational dimension, both in the relationship with others as equal or different, as well as in the relationship with one's own body; (3) a third level of *drive vicissitudes* from which derives the acting-out—or not—of sexuality; (4) a fourth level that regards roles and functions that are only secondarily and culturally determined; (5) a fifth *metaphoric* level, also much used in psychoanalytic theory (and to my mind the source of much confusion) that deals with "male" and "female" in an analogical, poetical, evocative sense, or as a composite dialectic duplicity of nature (Argentieri, 1988).

Although all these levels are closely interwoven, this does not mean that they are always harmoniously in step with each other during the course of development. Transvestism and transsexualism are the clamorous proof.

*Identification and disidentification: the levels of sexual identity.*

Regarding the acquisition of sexual identity, the problem of so-called "disidentification from the mother" is often mentioned, and there has always been substantial agreement on the conceptualizations expressed by Greenson (1968). Briefly, Greenson started from Freud's thesis, according to which the little girl has to elaborate two important conflictual areas that the little boy does not have to contend with: changing the erogenous zone from clitoris to vagina, and changing love object from mother to father. But, observes Greenson,

... the little boy, in order to reach a healthy sense of masculinity, must substitute his primary object of identification, the mother, and identify himself, instead, with the father. But I think that the difficulties inherent in this latter developmental step *from which little girls are exempt* are responsible for some special problems relative to the sexual identity of men ... The little girl, also, has to disidentify herself from the mother if she wants to develop her own personal feeling of self, but her identification with her mother helps her to establish her femininity. [Greenson, 1968, pp. 370–374, my italics]

For my part, I have many doubts about the supposed advantage that this so-called primary identification with the mother should have for feminine development. We may recall that Freud (1921c, 1923b) very rarely used the term "primary identification", referring to the "... most primitive form of affective bond with another person", a form of bond "in the pre-history of Oedipus" that is direct, immediate and does not provide for object investment; while secondary identifications, more tardy and structurizing, were, in his opinion, the result of introjective processes at the stage of the resolution of the Oedipus complex (Freud, 1923b).

It is true that, at the time of these Freudian conceptualizations, the very early events of development had not yet been described. But Freud did not fail to emphasize the archaic, pre-objectual non-sexual quality of this mechanism: "... in these primary identifications the ego copies ... the person" (Freud, 1921c); and later on he points out that we must distinguish between what the child wants to be (identification with the father) and what he wants to possess (the mother as sexual object investment) (*ibid.*).

Whatever our theoretic model of reference may be, I think we would all agree in confirming the difference (not only quantitative) between these early levels of so-called primary identification, of undifferentiation when the distinction between self and not-self has not yet taken place, and the successive levels of identity as a complex (even though never entirely completed) process of introjection, structurization, and integration.

Thus, by preserving the term of "primary identification" and the corresponding term of "disidentification", we continue to foster ambiguity and confusion; such as when we seem to take for granted that, for the little girl, the so-called primary identification with the mother is equivalent to a primitive kind of acquisition of feminine gender. (Argentieri, 1988) The difficult task that each one of us—whether male or female—has to face in order to acquire an identity, is, in fact, not one of disidentification, but of separation, individuation, and differentiation from the primary situation of fusion and undifferentiation with the mother, or, rather, with the parental figures. If this process is not satisfactorily accomplished, it is just as catastrophic for the development of the man as for the woman.

On the other hand, it is very difficult to understand how and when, during the course of development, gender identity, whether male or female, is inserted into and formed in the process of personal identity. It is true that everything starts from the corporeal, from very early sensorial experiences, and that, right from the very first stages of life when the boundary between self and the other has not yet been established, both boy and girl babies are able to mentally register intuitions and sensations about the difference between male and female; but I do not think that this must be considered either as being able to identify the mother as female, or to categorize in a morphologically adult, anatomical, and psychological sense the "male" and the "female". I think it is more acceptable to hypothesize that only in later stages, during the course of the separation, individuation, and differentiation processes, is there a re-categorization, in the form of a "retroactive effect", of the primitive experiences and fantasies in terms of male and female at more integrated levels (Fast, 1979).

Therefore, at the origins, at the phase of the so-called primary identifications (but also, as we learn from our clinical experience, in adult phases, if pathological developments have not allowed for an adequate maturation), the maternal image, rather than being "female", cannot be anything but confused and composed of characteristics and functions that are at the same time "maternal" and "paternal"; so that the mature acquisition of one's own sexual identity is always accompanied by the reciprocal recognition of that of the opposite sex. A man cannot really become a man without understanding what a woman is; similarly, in order to develop a female image, a little girl, beginning with her primary relationship with her mother, must develop a parallel sense of masculinity attributed to the actual males with whom she comes into contact.

The normal phases of female life, such as menarche, pregnancy, and breast-feeding, imply not only a moment of growth, but also the recognition of being concretely equal to the mother; and the more this relationship is burdened by ambiguity, above all of the mother towards the daughter who is growing up and who she feels is endangering her role of idealized mother, the more threatening this can be (Pine, 1992).

I think this is why many young girls feel that belonging to the female gender is like a trap, implying that they will be regressively recaptured forever by the very mother from whom they are desperately trying to detach themselves. Thus, the difficulty of emerging from the fusional bond is often expressed in pathologies regarding feminine gender identity, such as amenorrhea, sterility, miscarriages, or transsexualism.

In clear contrast with the conceptualizations based on Greenson, I think that the exact opposite is the case: that for the woman, the so-called primary identification, the undifferentiated, fusional level with the mother, far from being a help, can constitute the greatest obstacle for the acquisition of feminine gender identity.

Stoller speaks of a *primitive proto-femininity*, common to the little boy and to the little girl, to which the patient would remain anchored; while Person and Ovesey (1974a,b) (with whom I am in greater agreement on this point) refer to an ambiguous primitive nucleus that is not yet either male or female. We should add that the two sexophobic and sexophilic "opposite extremes"—all monsters/all normal—are also collusive allies in discouraging the pervert from spontaneously seeking for help and treatment. In the first case, fear and anger exalt the defence of the idealization and negation of the subject's pathology; in the second case, they represent a useful alibi for not changing.

A revealing sign of gender identity is, I think, *posture*: the way that transsexuals walk and move is so spontaneously similar to that of the desired sex that it seems to have been inscribed very early on into the corporeal image, in the bones and in the muscles. In contrast, there is the exaggerated emphasis of transvestites, the theatrical quality with which they show off their attitude in their bodies.

I give as an example the case of Caterina, twenty-two years old, a student in engineering. She comes for a consultation after an interrupted cognitive type of psychotherapy. "The things they asked me about my childhood didn't mean anything to me. I have other problems", she began, already discouraged. She has "always" known that there is something wrong with her feminine body. She has tried to find relief by making love with a woman, but it served no purpose; it was only gymnastics. "I'm not a lesbian!" she says indignantly.

Caterina is pleasant-looking, she dresses well and has long hair; she is not "coquettish" in any way, but neither does she show any macho characteristics. After the consultation, I accompany her to the door; as I follow her along the corridor, I notice her way of walking, which is more eloquent than any discourse. She moves exactly like a boy, and I realize that I am quite unable to help her in the only way she would like.

Another psychophysical aspect of sexual gender is the *voice*, but this deserves a paper to itself.

Naturally, we all wonder what the very early relations of these patients with their parents could have been. But I think that we must not place too much emphasis on the *genetic* aspect. We inevitably discover elements that are generic, not specific, and that can be found in any number of pathologies. I am thinking of the exasperating monotony of today's clinical accounts, all mentioning possessive mothers and absent fathers in almost every type of pathology in both sexes. It is obvious that transvestites and transsexuals have had an unresolved fusional relationship with the mother, and that the father has not adequately carried out his function of "third". But, unfortunately, this is not indicative, nor can it be indicated later on (in a mechanical *post hoc, propter hoc* connection) as the "cause" of particular syndromes.

Eugenio comes for a consultation for the first time when he is twenty-seven. He is an intelligent and sensitive young man, very well-educated. He himself relates his impulse to dress like a woman to the death of his mother, to whom he was very attached. However, he is not attracted to the typical showy "look" of transvestites; he prefers a "lady-like" style, simple and almost shabby. More explicitly still, he begins to wear his mother's clothes that he has devotedly preserved. His pleasure increases when, thus clothed, he goes shopping to look for new accessories. He says quite clearly that, for him, dressing up is an expedient for denying the pain of loss and avoiding mourning.

Only years later are we able to understand the profound meaning of the destructive narcissism, rooted in childhood in a strict
complicity with his mother, and aimed at excluding the father. The
woman had, in fact, substituted her husband with her son, and had
"spared" him the Oedipal conflict. Thus, in later years, he had taken
to attacking the masculine, adult part of himself.

Both Stoller in the 1960s, and Person and Ovesey at the beginning of the 1970s, agree that gender identity disorder is rooted in
very early relations. Stoller claims to have singled out a fairly typical family situation, with a father who is insignificant and a mother
who captures the son in a fusional web that produces an "a-conflictual consolidation of the primitive nucleus of *proto-feminine* gender
identity". On the other hand, Person and Ovesey speak about an
*extreme and very early form of separation anxiety*, evoked in the child
by premature and traumatic experiences of interruption of the
fusion with the mother, that produces the terror of falling into
pieces, along the lines of Winnicott's anxieties of catastrophic annihilation of the self (or Gaddini's non-integration anxieties).

The fantasy of being all one with the mother can coincide with
the defence organization of transsexual delusion in the male, but it
is my opinion that this cannot be used to explain female transsexualism. Attachment to a "primary identification", if we must continue
to call it this, must be correlated with the need to exclude another
quota of identity, that linked to drive levels. I believe that this
happens both in transsexuals as well as in transvestites, although in
a less devastating form. What is difficult is to understand is when
the perversion really concerns sexual and aggressive drive vicissitudes; or when, instead, under the appearance of adult and evolved
types of behaviour, much more primitive needs of fusion and
contact are hidden, at whose service sexuality can be put.

However, I do not think that the psychoanalytic investigations
relative to the vicissitudes of destructive narcissism diminish the
value of Oedipus as the organizing or disorganizing "core" of a
perverse pathology. The further back one investigates, in fact, the
more one comes up against separation anxieties in the basic, but
generic elements of psychism. Perhaps we must reconsider how the
two levels—Oedipal and pre-Oedipal—overlap each other; with
what "endowment" is the Oedipal crossroads reached; how have
the preceding developmental events taken place beginning with the

undifferentiated sensuality of primary self-erotism, and with the processes of separation–individuation and of primary identification–disidentification; and how have the first defence organizations been articulated regarding archaic anxieties of integration–non-integration, of loss of self and of annihilation.

In other words, we must once again try to explore the extent to which successive stages of growth have been conditioned by what happened before; but also, through a "retroactive effect", how much the "after" reorganizes and reconstitutes the sense of "before".

In my view, this is how sexuality maintains its importance as a structuring and characterizing element of perversion, also—and particularly—when it is sacrificed. At the end of the day, experience shows that within the ambit of transvestism and transsexualism there are cases with a typical perverse structure, as well as mixed cases, forms of passage that are more plastic and mobile. We may come across patients with borderline organizations, carriers of various kinds of perverse symptoms, such as those who occasionally go with prostitutes, or transvestites (sometimes paedophiles or sado-masochists) in whom the perverse traits are only symptoms.

For example, a man, forty-three years old, a specialized workman, married for three years and with two steady lovers and other occasional ones, comes to a consultation very worried. Since his wife has become pregnant, every now and then he feels an impulse to dress as a woman and go on to the street to prostitute himself. He chooses elderly men with whom he practises fellatio.

It seemed evident to me that his imminent paternity had brought about the decompensation of a precarious psychosexual identity that until then had been compensated by sexual acting-out that was more acceptable at the conscious level (Pazzagli, 1999).

Sometimes, during an analysis, one can observe the passage from a perverse manner of acting to hypochondriac suffering, or to drug-addicted behaviour; this has no transformative sense, but is only an economic type of oscillation within the sphere of an archaic and autarchic functioning. (Argentieri, 1994).

I think this was the case with a patient of mine who suffered from alopecia areata, vitiligo, and atypical crises of asthma. Every now and then he indulged in the habit of frequenting transvestites who practised fellatio on him. I think this was the expression of a displacing of intolerable tension that did not correspond to any structural change.

## Gender identity disorders and homosexuality

There is a current tendency to confuse homosexuality, transvestism, and transsexualism. Unfortunately, this confusion often also occurs within the spheres of psychology and psychoanalysis. In classical psychiatry, homosexuality was kept distinct from transvestism and transsexualism, although it, too, was numbered among the perversions. Freud, however, in contrast with the psychiatrists of his time and also with some psychoanalysts of the first and second generation, never placed homosexuality among the perversions.

Strictly speaking, homosexuality is not a psychoanalytic, but only a descriptive concept, corresponding to the conscious and phenomenological levels of so-called sexual choice, and tells us nothing about the organization of the underlying structure.

As I see it, in homosexuality—as in heterosexuality—there can be everything: neuroses, psychoses, perversions, and also normality, or, rather, the sufficient amount of normality that affective and relational vicissitudes of individuals and of couples allow for.

Homosexuality, once concealed and the object of painful interpersonal and intrapsychic conflicts, is today proclaimed and exhibited as a short-cut to identity and a kind of *passe-partout* explanation. I am referring to the many men and women who, by declaring "I am homosexual", try to conceal behind this apparent pseudoidentity all the problems they have with themselves and with others. These are often defence organizations that have nothing to do with sex and very little to do with gender identity. They want to load every conflict on to the general band-wagon of homosexuality, seen as being transgressive and in need of external persecution (unfortunately not difficult to find in reality) in order to deny internal persecution. Behind this, there can be everything or nothing, but above all there is confusion. The real problem lies not in the "I am homosexual", but in the "I am".

It is absurd to label a person as pathological simply because they are homosexual. On the contrary, not even the opposite is true: that being, or proclaiming oneself to be, homosexual is automatic protection from being diagnosed as pathological. They are the two sides of the same worthless medal of prejudice. In all this, the monstrosity (at least to my way of thinking) of encouraging gay patients to be treated by openly declared gay therapists is beginning to take hold.

A transvestite is not necessarily homosexual; in fact, he is more often heterosexual. Nor do I believe that street prostitutes, who seem to follow the laws of supply and demand rather than of desire, can be considered as testifying to an authentic "preference". Similarly, in practised and manifest homosexuality, the sense of gender identity can be very different: there are gays who can be effeminate or "macho", and who certainly do not correspond to the commonly-held categories of "active" and "passive".

A young man, ex-heroin addict, sieropositive, unemployed, lives with a Brazilian "viados" who has kept his penis and testicles, but who has had his breasts "done". When he is not prostituting, he dresses ambiguously. They have been living happily together for some time now. What kind of sexuality or gender identity can one speak about in this couple?

## Collusion: a new form of conformism

I think we must say quite clearly that reconstruction (or the politically correct "reattribution") is an illusion, or, better still, a fraud consisting of irreversible surgical devastation. It is a concrete splitting, by means of a scalpel. Fortunately, the patients themselves—crazy but not stupid—begin to realize this before the doctors do. As a young woman transsexual, desperate but lucid, said, "I don't want the operation: that is only a masquerade."

Certainly, problems of gender identity have always existed in all ages and cultures. Today, however, thanks to modern technology, it is possible to put into practice those eternal fantasies. In a kind of evil collusion with each other, the first responsible are the *doctors*—endocrinologists and surgeons—who have not the humility to admit the natural limitations of every therapeutic act. More or less in bad faith, perhaps at the preconscious level, and with a kind of "God complex", they arrogantly claim to create new identities on demand. As for *psychologists*, they are usually confined to the role of mere hangers-on in the team. Whatever kind of psychotherapy is possible when patients have already been told that, in order to be allowed medical–surgical treatment, they must first "elaborate" their wish to change sex? They risk being used by their clients solely to confirm what they, the clients, are already convinced about. *Psychoanalysts* generally limit themselves to intervening, when the damage has already been done, with refined but hesitant reflections, and keeping themselves out of the scrum. On the other hand, no one listens to them very much; for example, my suggestion that the psychological study groups should be made up not with the patients who want treatment, but with the medical–surgical team, had no follow-up.

If we take a step backwards in time, we see that *parents* and *relatives* (as we learn from the long and wise experience of Di Ceglie) feel inadequate to confront the sexual gender identity problems of their children at the time when they emerge. Incapable of exercising authority (as are the majority of adults these days), they are easily blackmailed by young pre-adolescents, both male and female, who threaten suicide and insist on being treated with the prerogatives of the opposite sex, beginning with the name, and have not the least intention of putting the matter up for discussion; it is the others who must adhere to their circumscribed delusion. Parents can thus in good faith become the paladins of the "free choice" of their offspring.

The most subtle collusion is, in fact, that of the *patients* themselves, who put all their energies at the service of their project; obstinately tenacious, they want to confine their discomfort to the body and will only accept treatment on the anatomical plane. In this sense, the role of the various "movements" of liberation, pride, solidarity, study, etc., is of prime importance. Thanks to the re-enforcing function of the group, the question moves on to the level of legal claims, and all the conflictuality is directed "outside" through aggressiveness and controversy against the repressive society.

An argument that I have often heard in support of surgery for changing sex is that these patients are, in any case, irremovable and are at high risk of suicide and psychotic breakdown. Although it is destructive, surgery could be the lesser risk. However, from my limited experience, I have seen that the need is not appeased. At first the suffering is eased, but when, after years of physical torture, psychological suffering, and financial sacrifices, they realize that "reconstruction", or, rather, "re-attribution", is impossible and that the demolition is irreversible, then they are consumed with anger, desperation, anxiety, and, above all, resentment for the deception they have suffered.

Other people think the alternative strategy could be used of permitting the change of sexual gender on *documents* without the necessary anatomical changes. This would certainly be less drastic, but it favours alliance with the defences rather than meeting the needs of the patient. The other defensive strategy consists of throwing all the cases of "neo-sexuality" together into the same melting-pot, and insistently using the question of homosexuality as an all-encompassing protective shield for demands of social recognition.

Clearly, on the phenomenological plane, problems of drive and of sex gender, of transvestism and transsexualism, of homo- and heterosexuality, can interweave and overlap in individual cases; but it is useless, in fact harmful, to confuse them also on the theoretical plane; for example, the common cliché that the "femininity" of gays makes them "less violent and more sympathetic", a kind of stereotyped equivalence between male homosexuals and women. Regarding homosexuals themselves, both male and female, there seems to be a variable response to these simplifications. Sometimes they encourage them, because it is an advantage to be allied with the numerical force of the new movements for the conquest of civil and cultural rights; at other times their reaction is one of embarrassment and rejection.

In all this not-so-innocent confusion, a good part of the responsibility lies with our present day culture, particularly—and unfortunately—that enlightened and progressive part of it that is terrorized by the idea of being accused of homophobia and racism that it immediately endorses every reductive ambiguity, hastily declaring solidarity at little expense to itself.

The Lacanian *Dizionario di Psicanalisi* (Chemama & Vandermersch, 2004), states that surgical sex changes are "a social psychosis that operates in the sexual dimension". For example, there is no point in talking about freedom of "choice" as far as our sexual orientation is concerned; if anything, it is we who "are chosen" by life to find more or less harmonious and happy solutions according to the life events and the relational history of each one of us. As a reaction to the brutal but explicit condemnation of the more conservative part of society, a *new conformism* has arisen: from moralistic condemnation to normalizing hypocrisy; from repression to collusion; two opposite ways of evading the responsibility of one's own opinion by taking refuge in a short-circuit of the senses. The same criticism applies to the use of biological argumentations: today, as yesterday, emphasizing the role of genes and chromosomes reduces the process of psychosexuality to a static, inevitable—and therefore not analysable—destiny.

The results of all this confusion are at the moment paradoxical and contradictory. Many "civilized" countries still do not recognize the rights of unmarried couples living together; marriages between non-traditional homo- and heterosexual couples, as well as adoptions, are spreading like wildfire; legal cases about sexual discrimination at work are arbitrary and episodic. On the other hand, change of sex through surgery is apparently universally accepted with no trouble. How is it that our society and our culture, usually so conservative and set in their ways, have declared themselves so open-minded on such a difficult theme? For example, in Australia, in Sydney, a judge has recently sanctioned the right of a girl of thirteen (!) to surgically "correct" her anatomical sex. Even in Iran, in 2004, the religious authorities who administer justice of a kind have decreed the legitimacy of such an operation. As for Italy, for over twenty years now the public health structures have provided for psychotherapy groups in preparation for hormone treatment and surgical manipulations.

I think that for most people it is less disturbing to proclaim their open-mindedness about surgical sex changes (based on the idea that they are a correction of nature's "mistake" on assumed biological genetic bases that are unchangeable, and thus eliminating the worrying psychological "disorder") than it is to really face up to homosexuality, a matter that concerns us all, with its relative complexities of life that certainly cannot be eliminated with a slice of the scalpel. All this takes place amid general an-affective confusion; in the malicious name of pseudo-liberal ideology, it is seen as a short-cut to avoid thinking and the effort of coherence and commonsense, but, in exchange, allows one to feel pleasantly mature and forward-looking at the expense of others.

## The grey zone

In our so-called welfare society, the grey zone of ambiguous situations, at the elusive limit between normality and pathology, are spreading out of all proportion, and only occasionally do we come across them in our psychoanalytic studios. I am thinking, for example, of the enormous—systematic or occasional—consumption of pornography, above all video pornography, with its various perverse nuances ranging from sadomasochism to paedophilia; of the visits to certain notorious websites, perhaps in the office, "by chance", for curiosity or boredom; of the alibi of using something that just "appears" in front of you without having explicitly wanted it, facilitated by the unemotional de-responsibility due to the remote and anonymous quality of the material in question The fear of direct sexual confrontation, as well as emotional apathy, make the homely comfort of these less involving forms of Eros preferable; the more so since the viewing is not even regularly accompanied by masturbation, and sometimes even bodily effort is avoided in favour of a mild excitation of the brain.

I think, too, of the horror of "sex tourism", or of the street and child prostitutes frequented by so many nice boys and fathers of families, who, by conveniently forgetting the cause–effect connection between demand and supply, and relegating the well-known data about violence and modern slavery to increasingly remote areas of their conscience, perpetuate, through their complicity, the harm that is done to the victims. All this takes place in a climate of "tolerance" of the distracted and unemotional violence of our age; within a framework of statistical pseudo-normality of things that are done by everyone—or at least by many.

Continuing with the list of changes, it is increasingly difficult nowadays to find the classical distinction between transsexual and transvestite. Such diagnostic criteria have certainly lost their meaning when applied to the "viados", with their mixture of poverty, commerce, and gender confusion; they would be of even less use in explaining the psychic set-up of their increasingly numerous clients, who, in many ways, could be absolutely "anyone". Also, in the bodies of these people "in transit", we see that a great mixture of solutions have been used; a patchwork of depilation and moustaches, artificial breasts and male genitals, intermittent hormones, etc.

I do not think that in any of these people could we find the typical structure of "splitting" that we singled out in the classical perversions; at most, it is micro-splitting or regressions to ambiguity that are at work and are by now endemic in the psychopathology of everyday life. Besides, the two famous differences of the Oedipal crossroads (between child and adult, and between male and female) nowadays have much less value; in the general defensive tendency towards undifferentation, they seem to be less significant for the construction of identity. All this facilitates the orientation towards a transvestite or transsexual organization in patients who must negotiate between anxieties and defence.

In such a confused picture, where the metapsychological parameters that were our guides until recently are missing, can we avoid evaluating as perverts anyone of those who are aroused by watching a video of a child being sodomized, simply because they do not have the classical psychic structure? Is the authority of numbers, statistical frequency and mass indifference sufficient to make all the "variations" normal?

I am aware that by broadening what I have called the "grey zone" I am exceeding the sphere of clinical competence of psychoanalysis. In this scenario are formed the trivial psychological traits so common to our affluent society: chronic unhappiness, resentment, psychological autarchy, the mean lack of self-affection that lurks inside those endless complaints about solitude, dependency on bodily sensations for finding one's own emotions, and, above all, the great misunderstanding of our age: that sex in the form of concrete sexual activity, and not as a means of encounter with another, can be the integrating mainstay of identity and the means for attaining happiness on earth.

## The role of psychoanalysis

The specificity of psychoanalysis regarding sexuality lies in the refusal to consider it as a "function" in itself, but as an integral part of the person in the relational dimension. We are not so much interested in the multi-coloured forms of Eros, but in the capacity to experience and to integrate in the interpersonal and intrapsychic dimension emotions and passions, sex and affects. As Balint said, the compass is not so much the sexual gender of the partner, but the degree of object relation and of recognition of the other in his/her entirety. It can be an indication of pathology, on the other hand, when there is obsession, or the compulsion to find concrete and anatomical solutions to unconscious conflicts and to human complexity.

Based on these premises, and as things stand at the moment in our country, it is unlikely that psychoanalysis can be of use to such patients as these. Seduction by those who offer remedies mirroring their omnipotent wishes is too strong; while we psychoanalysts can only bring to light the anxieties and share the pain of realizing that the wished-for solution does not exist. It is not our repressive society that is the enemy, but the reality principle to which we, as well as they, must submit.

I am not one who believes that psychoanalysis should be prescriptive or dominant, something that our discipline must not and cannot be. Nor do I feel any personal need to stigmatize life solutions, the negotiations between drives, anxieties and defences that everyone carries out in their own way according to the circumstances that life offers them. As Tolstoy says, he who is happy is always right. The trouble is that the cases I am speaking about are anything but happy.

A possible and reasonable objection to my argumentations is that probably, in their clinical work, psychoanalysts only come across cases that have had negative results and so are unaware of all those who, through the "change" of sex, have achieved, if not happiness, then at least internal tranquillity. It is true that those who come to me are the unhappy or uncertain cases; but my answer is that there are more than enough of them to justify alarm and my appeal for caution, and also my condemnation of the vein of madness perpetrated in the clinical environment with the blessing of the public health services.

I may add that I do not live closed up in my studio; I have met and, on public occasions, have argued in vain with those who refuse to give up the illusion and who, after repeated failures, continue to hold out the pathological hope of finding a new magic surgeon who will at last perform the miracle. I have also met people who, by using maniacal defences to the bitter end, flaunt the "success" of their treatment and are perpetually seeking for ideological accomplices and public compliance to applaud their triumph. Maniacal defences based on denial and splitting and emphasizing psycho-sensorial, imitative levels of contact, only serve to deny reality and its limits and to flee from depressive anxieties, thus acting as the flywheel to omnipotence.

On the other hand, it is inevitable (as I know to my cost) that a violent stream of verbal aggressiveness will be directed towards those who do not take sides; it is a conflict that I do not avoid—also on this occasion—because the transsexuals' need to be recognized in their own identity, to be "seen" just as they feel themselves to be, is an opportunity for dialogue that must not be wasted.

## Analysability and curability

Taking into account all these reflections and acquisitions, the final question—and also the most relevant from the clinical point of view—is: nowadays, do we still agree with the strict affirmation of the "classical" psychoanalysts that patients such as these are untreatable? Even if they do come to be treated, are they analysable? Are they curable? For what the numerically slight experience of a single analyst may be worth, I can say that I have had, in analysis and in psychotherapy, both perverse patients with the classical structure of denial and splitting, and patients with more or less serious perverse symptomatic traits, in both cases with varying final results.

As an example, in the case of psychotherapy with a "classical" perverse patient, I have watched bitterly as the healthy part and the psychotic part have grown alongside each other, nourished by the analysis. Precisely because the patient's personality has been formed on the basis of the typical structure, it is relatively stable; difficult to modify because denial and splitting, as we know, safeguard from complete psychosis. Certainly, this patient is definitely analysable; I could not say whether curable or, if not curable, whether this depends on the pathology or on my relative inexperience. The treatment is still going on and I base my hopes on the patient's need of a "public" to be present at his triumph, as Zucconi says.

Regarding the many cases with occasional traits and symptoms, the difficulties and uncertainties about the outcome of the cure seem to me to be exactly the same as those we come across with other narcissistic and borderline patients who were once considered unanalysable but who, today, are almost the daily bread of all of us. It is no less difficult to decide whether the disappearance of the symptom is a positive sign of the analytic process, or whether, as in so many other unhealthy circumstances, it is only an oscillation that is insignificant from the point of view of development. On the other hand, the criteria used to indicate an analysis and to establish recovery are among the most slippery and controversial. We can only continue to try.

Following this line of thought, the diagnosis of a perversion, "true" or symptomatic, becomes less significant compared with the need to analyse how and when the patient has substituted the mutual freedom of the sexual relationship complete with its emotions, affects and passions, with a modality of self-coercion, mental rather than physical, leading to extreme degrees of humiliation and violence. The common denominator (certainly generic, but in any case more important) of the various pathologies is self-referentiability and the non-recognition of otherness. Besides, even in the most banal and marginal forms of "transgressive" sexuality, such as occasionally going with male or female prostitutes, is certainly not a question of "conceding oneself a liberty", but of indulging in (and what is more, often at the expense of someone else's freedom) "partial" and coercive forms of erotism that evade the completeness of the encounter with the self and with the other. My aim, in fact, is not to make them change their ideas, or even to "redeem" them or "cure" them, but only to bring their drama back on to symbolic ground instead of being chained to the concreteness of the flesh.

I am wary of those who claim to make a defensive shell out of their sexual behaviour, as though presenting a hetero couple were a guarantee of sanity and normality. But I am also wary of those who like to parade their own personal atypical solution. I know that, often, the ego's needs for pleasure can prevail over the id's needs for security, and that in order to guarantee tranquillity and stability many people prefer to sacrifice their libido. We all do what we can.

As we learn from Di Ceglie's long experience, the task of a psychoanalyst, whether requested through an analysis or a consultation, can only be that of helping each person to tolerate doubt, ambiguity, uncertainty; of allowing time for understanding one's own anxieties instead of seeking flight towards enactment. If they will allow us to, we may assist those who are suffering from uncertainty about their sexual gender to tolerate the doubt, to bear the limits that reality opposes to the narcissistic pretence of being "everything"; to find an individual adjustment between anxieties and defences that is less destructive and more congenial to them; to improve the relationship with their own body and with others. Or else we can adopt the expected and quite legitimate solution of standing aside, as psychoanalysts and psychotherapists, as far as their destiny is concerned, and renouncing our claim to know better than they do what they must do, how they must appear, who they must love. What we must not do, however, is to endorse the misunderstanding that a biological "mistake" of nature lies at the root of their destiny, and that the solution is to be carried out on the body by violating it with scalpels and hormones. As the anthropologist Carla Pasquinelli (personal communication) says, we must beware of any operation legitimizing cultural judgement in the guise of naturalness.

## Summary

During the course of a few decades, there has been a dramatic change, both psychologically and in civil rights, in the convulsive social and cultural arena in which the so-called "transsexualisms" live, define themselves, and are defined. Even the technical language has changed. In the past, diagnoses of transsexualism and transvestism were quite distinct from each other; whereas, today, we speak of "gender dysphoria", or we use the comprehensive term of "transgender" that moves the accent from sexual drive to gender identity. In our clinical work, the phenomenon of so-called infantile "cross-dressing" has increased, and there are many more cases of feminine perversions, or, at least, their existence is no longer denied, although they may go under different names.

I think that psychoanalysis must make the effort to retrieve its theoretical space and its specific method of clinical operation so as to remove it from the confused scandals of the media, and from the collusive, falsely liberal seduction of medical–surgical

"re-attribution" of sexual gender (now permitted in the public institutions of many countries) that, in fact, puts the problem back on
the biological level. We cannot limit ourselves, as frequently
happens, to intervening when the damage has already been done.

We have to understand whether the actual psychological organizations of transsexuals and transvestites correspond to the structural hypotheses formulated by Freud in his time; and how, from
time to time, the compromise of the very early, pre-oedipal levels
relative to the construction of gender identity interweaves with that
of the sexual oedipal and drive levels.

It is also important to understand analytically the relational
dynamics of those who accompany, love, or sometimes sexually
exploit transvestites and transsexuals, in the "grey zone" on the
boundaries of so-called normality. Furthermore, the specificity of
psychoanalysis regarding sexuality is to consider it not as a "function" in itself, but as an integrating part of the person. According to
our discipline, it is not the descriptive, phenomenological aspects of
sexuality that determine maturity, but the entire object relationship
that each individual manages to establish with the other.

## Note

1.  Translated by Jill Whitelaw Cucco.

## References

Argentieri, S. (1988). Il sesso degli angeli. In: AA VV *Del genere sessuale*.
   Roma: Borla.
Argentieri, S. (1991). Dal corporeo e dal preverbale alla parola:
   trascrizioni possibili e impossibili in psicoanalisi. Atti del Convegno
   "Le Riscritture" del Centro Romano di Semiotica, Roma.
Argentieri, S. (1994). Malattie psicosomatiche e perversioni. Atti del
   Congresso "Le Malattie psicosomatiche in età evolutiva", Milano,
   1992. Arca di Como editore.
Bion, W. (1957). Differentiation of the psychotic from the non psychotic
   personalities. *International Journal of Psychoanalysis, 38*: 266–275.
Chemama, R., & Vandermersch, B. (2004). *Dizionario di Psicanalisi*.
   Roma: Gremese [original version: R. Chemama & B. Vandermersch
   (Eds.), *Dictionnaire de la psychanalyse*. Paris: Larousse, 1998].

Chiland, C. (2000). The psychoanalyst and the transsexual patient. *International Journal of Psychoanalysis, 81*: 21–35.

Chiland, C. (2003). *Le transsexualisme*. Paris: Presses Universitaires de France.

Cooper, A. M. (1991). Perversions and near-perversions. In: G. Fogel & W. Myers (Eds.), *Clinical Practice: New Psychoanalytic Perspective*. New Haven, CT: Yale University Press.

Fast, I. (1979). Developments in gender identity: gender differentiation in girls. *Journal of Psychoanalysis, 60*(4): 443–454.

Freud, S. (1921c). Group psychology and the analysis of the ego. *S.E., 18*: 69.

Freud, S. (1923b). *The Ego and the Id. S.E., 19*: 3.

Green, A. (1986). *On Private Madness*. London: Hogarth.

Greenson, R. R. (1968). Disidentifying from mother: its special importance for the boy. *International Journal of Psychoanalysis, 49*: 370–374 (edizione italiana in: *Esplorazioni psicoanalitiche*. Torino: Boringhieri, 1984).

Kaplan, L. J. (1991). *Female Perversions*. New York: Doubleday.

Khan, M. (1979). *Le figure della perversione*. Torino: Bollati Boringhieri, 1982.

Limentani, A. (1977). Clinical types of homosexuality. In: *Between Freud and Klein*. London: Free Association, 1989.

Limentani, A. (1979). The significance of transsexualism in relation to some basic psychoanalytic concepts. *International Review of Psycho-Analysis, 6*: 139–153.

Molfino, F. (1995). Seduzione del padre, seduzione della madre. In *AA.VV., Corpo a corpo*, Laterza, Bari.

Oppenheimer, A. (1991). The wish for a sex change: a challenge to psychoanalysis? *International Journal of Psycho-Analysis, 72*: 221–231.

Pasquinelli, C. Personal communication.

Pazzagli, A. (1999). Il travaglio della paternità. In: S. Argentieri (Ed.), *Il padre materno. Da San Giuseppe ai nuovi mammi*. Rome: Meltemi.

Person, E., & Ovesey, L. (1974a). The transsexual syndrome in males. I. Primary transsexualism. *American Journal of Psychotherapy, 28*: 4–20.

Person, E., & Ovesey, L. (1974b). The transsexual syndrome in males. II. Secondary transsexualism. *American Journal of Psychotherapy, 28*: 174–193.

Pine, D. (1992). The relevance of early psychic development to pregnancy and abortion. *International Journal of Psychoanalysis, 63*: 311–318.

Quinodoz, D. (1998). A female transsexual patient in psychoanalysis. *International Journal of Psychoanalysis, 79*: 95–111.

Socarides, C. W. (1970). A psychoanalytic study of the desire for sexual transformation ('transsexualism'): the Plaster-of-Paris man. *International Journal of Psychoanalysis*. 51: 341–349.

Stoller, R. (1968). *Sex and Gender*. New York: Science House.

Whitebook, J. (1991). Perversion: destruction and reparation: on the contribution of J. Chasseguet-Smirgell and J. McDougall. *American Imago*, 48(3): 329–350.

## Bibliography

Amati Mehler, J. (1992). Love and male impotence. *Int. J. Psycho-Anal.*, 73: 467–480.

Amati Mehler, J. (1999). Perversioni: struttura, sintomo o meccanismo? *Psicoanalisi*, 3(1): 59. Roma: Il Pensiero Scientifico Editore.

Amati Mehler, J., Argentieri, S., & Canestri, J. (2004). *La Babele dell'inconscio: Lingua madre e lingue straniere nella dimensione psicoanalitica - nuova edizione* (cap. "Identità e identità di genere attraverso le lingue" cap. IV), Milano Raffaello Cortina Editore.

Argentieri, S. (1982a) Anna Freud, la figlia. In: S. Vegetti Finzi (Eds.), *Psicoanalisi al femminile*. Laterza, Roma-Bari.

Argentieri, S. (1982b). Sui processi mentali precoci dell'identità femminile. In: *Rivista di Psicoanalisi*, XXVIII, 3. Roma: Il Pensiero Scientifico editore.

Argentieri, S. (1985). Sulla cosiddetta disidentificazione dalla madre. In: *Rivista di Psicoanalisi*, XXXI, 3. Roma: Il Pensiero Scientifico editore.

Argentieri, S. (1993). More than one analyst in the family—Sigmund and Anna Freud. *IPA Newsletter*, 2.

Argentieri, S. (1995). Riflessioni sul destino di un evirato cantore. In: Sandro Cappelletto *La voce perduta. Vita di Farinelli, evirato cantore*. Torino: EDT.

Argentieri, S. (1999). *Il padre materno. Da San Giuseppe ai nuovi mammi*. Roma: Meltemi.

Argentieri, S. (2000). La malafede come nevrosi e come crimine. *Psicoanalisi*, 4(2), Roma: Il Pensiero Scientifico editore.

Argentieri, S. (2001). La perversione della civiltà. *Micromega*, 4, 2001.

Argentieri, S. (2003). The ambiguity of bisexuality in psychoanalysis. In: A. M. Alizade (Ed.), *Studies on Femininity*. London: Karnac.

Argentieri, S. (2004). Perversioni o parafilie? Dal disagio della civiltà alla patologia del benessere. *Gli Argonauti*, anno IV, n. 7, giugno 2004. CIS editore, Milano.

Argentieri, S. (2005a). Incest yesterday and today: from conflict to ambiguity. In: G. Ambrosio (Ed.), *On Incest: Psychoanalytic Perspectives*. Pychoanalysis & Women Series - International Psychoanalytical Association. London: Karnac.

Argentieri, S. (2005b). La questione del transgender tra diritto e delirio. Intervento al Convegno "Trasformazioni del corpo e dignità della persona" della "Fondazione Basso". Roma: Maggio.

Argentieri, S. (2006). Transessualità, neosessualità: un nuovo conformismo. In: Nunziante Cesaro A. e Valerio P. (a cura di), *Dilemmi dell'identità: chi sono? —Saggi psicoanalitici sul genere sessuale*. Milano: F. Angeli editore.

Benjamin, H. (1966). *The Transsexual Phenomenon*. New York: Julian Press.

Bleger, J. (1967). *Simbiosis y ambigüedad, estudio psicoanalítico*. Buenos Aires: Editorial Paidos (trad. ital. 1992, *Simbiosi e ambiguità, studio psicoanalitico*, Libreria Editrice Lauretana, Loreto, Ancona).

Bolognini, S. (1998). Rassegna su "Psicoanalisi e sessualità". 40 Congresso Internazionale IPA, Barcellona, 1997. *Rivista di Psicoanalisi*, 1998, XLIV; 1. Borla editore.

Britton, R. (1989). The missing link: parental sexuality in the Oedipus complex. In: J. Steiner (Ed.), *The Oedipus Complex Today*. London: Karnac.

Carratelli, T. (1995). Transfert e trasmissione della vita psichica tra generazioni, intervento alla "Tavola Rotonda" *Il mito di Edipo rivisitato* del Convegno ASNE-SIPSIA 11 novembre 1995, Roma.

Castoldi, A. (1994). *Clérambault, stoffe e manichini*. Bergamo: Moretti e Vitali.

Cohen-Kettenis, P., & Pfäfflin, F. (2003). *Transgenderism and Intersexuality in Childhood and Adolescence. Making Choices*. Thousand Oaks, CA: Sage.

Copi "Il ballo delle checche", edizioni ES 1977.

De Simone, G. (2002). *Le famiglie di Edipo*. Roma: Borla.

De Simone, M. (2005). "Silenziosa voce" (in corso di pubblicazione).

Désirat, K. (1985). *Die transsexuelle Frau*. Stuttgart: Enke.

Di Ceglie, D. (Ed.) (1989). *In My Own Body. Atypical Gender Identity*. London: Karnac.

Di Ceglie, D., & Freedman, D. (Eds.) (1998). *A Stranger In My Own Body: Atypical Gender Identity Development and Mental Health*. London: Karnac.

Freud, S. (1905d). Three essays on the theory of sexuality. *S.E.*, 7: 125–245.

Freud, S. (1910h). A special type of choice object made by men, *S.E.*, *11*: 165.

Freud, S. (1912d). On the universal tendency to debasement in the sphere of love. *S.E.*, *11*: 179.

Freud, S. (1927e). Fetishism. *S.E.*, *21*: 149.

Freud, S. (1931b). Female sexuality. *S.E.*, *21*: 223.

Funghi, P., & Giunta, F. (Eds.) (2005). *Medicina, bioetica e diritto*. Pisa: ETS edizioni.

Gaddini, E. (1977). Formazione del padre e scena primaria. *Riv. Psicoanal.*, *23*, 2.

Gaddini, E. (1989). *Scritti - 1953–1985*. Milan: Raffaello Cortina Editore.

Garber, M. (1992). *Interessi truccati*. Milan: R. Cortina editore, 1994.

Green, R. (1987). *The "Sissy Boy Syndrome" and the Development of Homosexuality*. New Haven, CT: Yale University Press.

Greenson, R. R. (1978). Un bambino transessuale ed un'ipotesi. In: *Esplorazioni psicoanalitiche*. Torino: Bollati Boringhieri, 1984.

Limentani, A. (1966). A re-evolution of acting out in relation to working-trough. *International Journal of Psychoanalysis*, *47*: 274–285.

Lopez, D. (1970). *Analisi del carattere ed emancipazione—Marx, Freud, Reich*. Milano.

Lorand, S., & Balint, M. (1982). *Perversioni sessuali*. Milano: Feltrinelli.

Mistura, S. (a cura di) (2003). *Figure del feticismo*. Turin: Einaudi.

Mitchell, J. (1997). Sexuality, psychoanalysis and social change. *IPA News Letter*, *6*(1).

Nunziante, C. A., & Valerio, P. (Eds.) (2006). *Dilemmi dell'identità: chi sono?—Saggi psicoanalitici sul genere sessuale*. Milano: F. Angeli editore.

Person, E. (2001). Response to Juliet Mitchell's reflections. *Studies in Gender and Sexuality*, *2*: 261–275.

Petronio, G. (1987). Esibizionismo e voyeurismo. Paziente e analista allo specchio. *Gli Argonauti*, marzo 1987, n. 32. Milan: CIS editore.

Pfäfflin, F. (1983). Probleme der psychotherapeutischen Behandlung transsexueller Patienten. *Psychotherapie, Psychosomatik, medizinische Psychologie*, *3*: 89–92.

Pfäfflin, F. (1992). Regrets after sex reassignment surgery. *Journal of Psychology and Human Sexuality*, *5*: 69–85.

Pfäfflin, F. (1994). Zur transsexuellen Abwehr. *Psyche*, *48*: 904–931.

Pfäfflin, F. (1997). Sex reassignment, Harry Benjamin, and some European roots. *International Journal of Transgenderism*, *1*(2), www.symposion.com/ijt/ijtco2o2.htm.

Pfäfflin, F. (2003). Understanding transgendered phenomena. In: S. Levine (Ed.), *Handbook of Clinical Sexuality for Mental Health Professionals* (pp. 291–310). New York, Hove: Brunner-Routledge.

Pfäfflin, F., & Junge, A. (1998). Sex reassignment: thirty years of international follow-up studies. A comprehensive review, 1961–1991. *International Journal of Transgenderism*, book section. www.symposion.com/ijt/books/index.htm.

Quinodoz, D. (2002). Termination of a fe/male transsexual patient's analysis. An example of general validity. *International Journal of Psychoanalysis, 83*: 783–798.

Ruitenbeek, H. M. (a cura di) (1968). *Psicoterapia delle perversioni.* Astrolabio editore.

Sandler, J. (1981). *La ricerca in psicoanalisi,* Vol. II. Torino: Bollati Boringhieri.

Stoller, R. (1975). *The Transsexual Experiment. Sex and Gender,* Vol. II. London: Hogarth Press.

Stoller, R. J. (1985). *Observing the Erotic Imagination.* New Haven, CT: Yale University Press.

Thomä, H. (1957). Männlicher transvestitismus und das verlangen nach geschlechtsumwandlung. *Psyche, 11*: 81–124.

Toraldo di Francia, M. (2002). I dilemmi etici della medicina contemporanea: In: AA. VV., *Cure di fine vita.* Salute e territorio, n.134, 2002, pp. 300ss.

Tyszler, J. J. (1996). La pelle rivoltata. Note sul godimento di involucro" In: P. Valerio, M. Bottone & R. Vitelli (Eds.), *Transessualismo. Saggi psicoanalitici.* Milan: F. Angeli, 2001.

Valerio, P., Bottone, M., Galiani, R., & Vitelli, R. (Eds.) (2001). *Il transessuale. Saggi psicoanalitici.* Milan: F. Angeli.

Welldon, E. V. (1988). *Mother, Madonna, Whore. The Idealisation and Denigration of Motherhood.* London: Free Association.

Welldon, E. V. (1991). *Un punto di vista psicoanalitico sulle perversioni femminili.* Freud Memorial Lecture, London University (trad. italiana in "Quaderni ASP, anno 2, n. 7, 1993, Milan).

Whitebook, J. (1995). *Perversion and Utopia—A Study in Psychoanalysis and Critical Theory.* Cambridge, MA: MIT Press.

Winnicott, D. W. (1956). On transference. *Journal of Psychoanalysis, 37*: 386–388.

Zucconi, S. (2004). L'amore perverso. In: *Gli Argonauti,* anno IV, n. 7, giugno 2004. Milan: CIS editore.

Zucker, K., & Bradley, S. (1995). *Gender Identity Disorder and Psychosexual Problems in Children and Adolescents.* New York: Guilford.

# CHAPTER TWO

# Some thoughts on transsexualism, transvestism, transgender, and identification[1]

*Colette Chiland*

Only a few psychoanalysts have any experience with transvestism, transsexualism, and transgenderism. Our discussants are usually doctors and psychologists who deal with sex reassignment and hormono–surgical transformation, people to whom our psychoanalytic concerns mean little. The COWAP meeting in Catania gave us the opportunity to discuss these topics between psychoanalysts.

In this chapter, I shall focus on issues on which my own experience can shed some light.

We have set up a small team of psychoanalysts to try to offer psychoanalytic treatment to transsexuals and transvestites: most of the time this will be psychotherapy, very rarely psychoanalysis in the full sense of the word. When I say that we try to offer this, I mean that few of these patients actively seek this kind of help or believe in its usefulness. It is true also that, financially speaking, some are simply not in a position to pay expensive fees which are not refunded by the social security system. We try to find solutions appropriate to each particular case.

In addition to treatment *stricto sensu*, I have been consulted by many patients (children and their parents, adolescents, and adults), either referred to me or who have come on their own initiative for my opinion; we could therefore say that my experience in this field is extensive, if not particularly in-depth. More specifically, I conducted a catamnestic study of forty-nine patients who had undergone an operation. In a CECOS (Egg and Sperm Research and Preservation Centre), I have seen more than forty couples in which the men were female-to-male transsexuals; they came to the Centre requesting artificial insemination by donor for the woman member of the couple.

## Nosological labels

Of course it is not the nosological label as such that is the major issue here, but our understanding of how the individual's mind works. From that point of view, transvestites are different from transsexuals, as Simona Argentieri (Chapter One) suggests, and as we shall see shortly. However, rather than speak in terms of clear-cut categories, I have chosen the idea of "components": identity component, transvestite component and sexual component (which in earlier texts I called homosexual component). In his discussion of the neuroses, Freud pointed out that there were many more mixed cases than pure ones.

## The identity component

Transsexuals, *stricto sensu*, are people in whom the identity component is the dominant factor: they simply cannot live with/in the male (or female) body with which they were born (they are not intersex: our present methods of investigation do not reveal any biological component typical of the opposite sex). The issues involved are dramatic and existential, which is why I have used the term "an illness of narcissism": these individuals have never managed to build up a sense of continuity of their self, of ongoing being, they have no self-esteem, they are unable to love and to be loved except as members of the opposite sex. They cannot conceive of any solution other than hormones and surgery in order to "change their sex".

But is it possible to change one's sex? I have been the target of attacks—of sheer hatred—because I have maintained that the idea of changing one's sex is a mad one, since it is in itself impossible. As to that impossibility, Simona Argentieri and I are in agreement. No medical practitioner would ever say what journalists write: "Nowadays, a man can be changed into a woman, a woman into a man". All that can be changed is the appearance of that person's body—sometimes very convincingly—and civil status; the inside of the body (chromosomes, internal genital organs) remains the same. Nor can we erase the past history of the person concerned, although transsexuals want so much to do this that they say they have no memories of their childhood; they manage to wipe out all memory traces more by denial and splitting than by repression.

Those who have "changed their sex", have undergone the requisite operation, and have obtained a modification of their civil status express a whole range of views.

Asking for "their body to be harmonized with their soul" can cover many different points of view. When they express that request in terms of "restoring their true body", it has a particular quality to it. Some state categorically (or insist on doing so: some do actually believe this, while others manifest a defensive kind of bravado) that henceforth they (formerly men) are now women or (formerly women) are now men. Some patients have told me that their neo-sex is proof of their sex change: "When I look at myself in the mirror, my phalloplasty is proof that I am speaking the truth when I say that I am a man". The false penis is proof that the person is a true man. (A phalloplasty is not a functional penis and does not really look like one.) That kind of statement is in line with what Simona Argentieri writes, "a typical circumscribed delusion". I cannot, however, go along with her when she goes on to generalize, saying, "In my experience, *the psychopathological organization of transsexualism is substantially* the same in men as in women: *the delusional conviction (a typical circumscribed delusion) of belonging to the opposite sex*" (my italics).

Many acknowledge—and it is painful for them to do so—that after the operation they are not in every respect comparable to men born as men or to women born as women, and this upsets them. Some go as far as to say, "Since doctors are unable to give us the real body of the opposite sex, we'll have to change what's in our

minds". Therein lies the justification for our work as psychoanalysts. I shall come back later to the question of treatment outcome.

Some say, "I live as a woman and I'm happy about that, even
though my dream of being a fully-fledged woman is an impossible
one". That is obviously quite a different attitude.

It is obvious, then, that these different points of view cannot
all be put in the same basket and taken simply to be delusion and
psychosis, even less of perversion, although the presence of denial
and splitting has to be acknowledged.

### The transvestite component

Basically, the transvestite component concerns males and only
males. Throughout his career, Stoller encountered only three cases
of female transvestites, that is, women who experience an intense
erotic pleasure by dressing up as men. Argentieri, too, writes, "I do
not think I have ever come across any real cases of transvestism in
females". Thus, we are in agreement on that point.

Transsexuals feel "comfortable" when they wear women's clothing because this gives them the appearance of being women and
thus corresponds to their intimate feeling of actually being women.
For some, however, there is something more than just feeling comfortable; they really do experience an intense pleasure of a sexual
nature. Being attracted to women's clothes is a significant component of their identity as women. They do not want simply to be a
woman, they want to be the most beautiful woman of all, the most
desirable. I have seen boys who refused to be boys caressing the
fabric of their mother's wedding-gown or the hair of a Barbie doll
in a near-orgasmic state of ecstasy.

Others have initially been transvestites as described in clinical
reports: secret cross-dressers, dressed as women and masturbating
in front of a mirror; then, becoming bolder, going out into the world
and meeting other transvestites; in their life as men, they marry
(some tell their wife about their taste for cross-dressing), and
during intercourse they imagine themselves as having the woman's
role; then, one day, perhaps because their sexual potency begins to
decline, this is no longer enough for them, they want to become a
woman; at that point, their existential language is the same as that

of transsexuals, although it is only recently that the identity component has come to the fore.

On several occasions in her paper, Argentieri mentions the concept of perversion. It applies to transvestites through their search for sexual ecstasy and their manipulation of other people. According to Stoller, these individuals were themselves manipulated as children, cross-dressed and made fun of by some woman or other in their immediate circle; their perversion in adulthood is an active and triumphant revenge for the humiliation they then endured. That way of looking at the situation can help us cope with the negative countertransference that perverse people evoke in us.

## The sexual component

It was said that "true transsexuals" have no sexual desire. And some transsexuals try not to show any sexual desire so that they could be considered as "true transsexuals" and be operated on.

When they speak of their desires, the male-to-female transsexuals usually say they have desire for a man, and the female-to-male transsexuals usually say they have desire for a woman. In the literature, these desires were spoken of as "homosexual". But the transsexuals do not feel themselves to be homosexuals. They say, "I am a woman, it is natural that I desire a man" (male-to-female transsexuals, mtf) or, "I am a man. It is natural that I desire a woman" (female-to-male transsexuals, ftm). Some mtf are attracted by women and say, "I am a lesbian", and some ftm are attracted by men and say, "I am a gay".

While waiting for the transformation, some mtf try to pick up men and have intercourse in which their penis plays no part; they do not want to be caressed or sucked off; they agree to anal intercourse, with their anus being used as a substitute for a vagina; they want their partner to treat them as a woman. Others wait until they have been given a neo-vagina before having sex.

In some cases of people who seek hormono–surgical sex reassignment, there is a genuine homosexual current. In adolescence, psychotherapy might help them take their homosexuality on board and give up the idea of transformation.

In girls, being sexually attracted to another girl is often at the heart of their discovery of themselves as transsexual. "Being attracted to girls is abnormal. I'm normal. So, if I'm attracted to girls, I must be a boy." Female-to-male transsexuals often come to a specialist consultation as a couple. Their sexuality, however, is only exceptionally of a homosexual nature, with reciprocal caressing: they do not show themselves naked to their partner, nor do they want their partner to touch their breasts or clitoris; they want their partner to have pleasure; they themselves will have this experience later, after the operation.

When, after the operation, they live with their partner or wife, the latter is not homosexual; she will previously have had partners who were male and heterosexual. She cathects the female-to-male transsexual as a man, whom she loves, a man who is more gentle and more caring than those she knew previously. One such woman said to me, in a thoughtful and moving tone of voice, "My husband is not a woman. He is not a man like any other man—he is *a constructed man."*

I cannot be quite as clear with regard to the partners of male-to-female transsexuals, since I have not had the same opportunity of discussing the issues with couples in which the partner was ready for such an investigation.

Argentieri writes: "Transsexualism . . . provides only the desperate and extreme solution of sacrificing sexuality together with the part of the body that represents it". No, transsexuals do not give up their sexuality. Male-to-female transsexuals sometimes say, "Now I can experience a woman's orgasm"—an astonishing statement. Since their identity is that of a woman, what they experience, in their opinion, cannot but be a woman's orgasm, even if their body is constructed differently from that of women. As for the couple in which one partner is a female-to-male transsexual, there is an experience of sexual satisfaction, point taken, even though we may be tempted to think that their sexuality is incomplete and would not be particularly satisfying for us; what is important is what they experience and the happiness they can derive from that.

## Male-to-female and female-to-male transsexuals

To return to the extract from Argentieri's chapter which I began discussing earlier: "In my experience, *the psychopathological organization of transsexualism is substantially the same in men as in women*: the delusional conviction (a typical circumscribed delusion) of belonging to the opposite sex" (my italics). No, I do not agree! The psychopathological structure of male-to-female and female-to-male transsexuals is not "substantially the same", *mutatis mutandis*, as Freud might have said. That is a statement of fact, which is not easy to explain, but each situation is not a symmetrical replica of the other.

It is almost as though male-to-female transsexuals could be divided into two sub-groups, one of which resembles that of female-to-male transsexuals with regard to their level of intelligence, academic success, social and professional integration, and overall equilibrium; the other sub-group is more pathological, to such an extent that we could perhaps speak of "co-morbidity". In the catamnestic study that I carried out, ten out of twenty-two operated male-to-female transsexuals (45%) were receiving financial support from the state, as against one out of twenty-seven operated female-to-male transsexuals (2%), and even here the person concerned was only temporarily out of a job.

It would seem that refusing maleness and refusing femaleness are not of the same nature as far as the structure of the mind is concerned.

Rejecting maleness is the refusal of activity that is inevitably likened to aggressiveness. In a series of in-depth discussions with the parents of a boy who rejected his sex assignment as a male, they compared virility with aggressiveness; our hypothesis was that, very early on in their son's life, they had communicated to him their feelings about this through their emotions, their facial expressions, and their overall attitude, thereby discouraging him from manifesting anything that was "boyish" in nature. Boys who have been feminized in this way find themselves constantly wanting to be sexually desirable.

Rejecting femaleness is the refusal of passivity experienced as an out-and-out stigma. Often mothers of girls who reject their sex assignment have been depressed and belittled by their immediate circle simply because they are women. As girls become more masculine, they feel bound to prove themselves and become masters of their own fate.

Freud attached so much value to the penis that a male-to-female transsexual's request to have that organ removed almost amounts to the unimaginable crime of *lèse-majesty* with respect to Freud. If we follow his argument, we would expect penis envy to be upper-most in the female-to-male transsexual's request, but this is not, in fact, the case. Some female-to-male transsexuals are prepared to risk their life in doubtful operations in order to obtain a phallo-plasty with which to penetrate their partner. But, for most of them, what counts is their identity, not the phalloplasty, a mere semblance that for some has the value of a symbol. Identity involves identifi-cation with the masculine and paternal values of a given culture, and that is something which a "constructed man" can undoubtedly succeed in doing.

One of the things that surprised me in my work was the fact that I had the same experience as Stoller: he said that the first female-to-male transsexual he came across was not, contrary to his expecta-tion, a "butch homosexual" but a man—quite simply, a man—and during the eight years Stoller treated him he did not change his mind on that point (Stoller, 1985)

For my part, this made me think deeply about identification, and I shall compare my thoughts on this with what Argentieri says in her paper.

### Identification

Argentieri speaks of "sexual identity". In my view, that way of putting things should be avoided; it has become ambiguous in that it is often employed to designate sexual orientation. The relevant term in English is "gender identity"; in French, the term I use is *"identité sexuée"*, which could be translated into English as "sexed identity"; although we do come across this term from time to time, it is not (or not yet) in common use. I would argue that identity is always sexed: there is no such thing as a primary neuter and sexless identity which later becomes sexed. One's identity begins in the mind of one's parents, and no parent could ever bring up a "neuter" child: the intersex newborn for whom there is much hesitation about assigning a sex cannot in any circumstances be raised as if he or she were "neuter", as Rajon has shown in her excellent article (1998).

Freud wrote (1921c), "A little boy will exhibit a special interest in his father; he would like to grow like him and be like him, and take his place everywhere. We may say simply that he takes his father as his ideal" (p. 105). This is a conscious form of imitation, the aim of which is by "doing like" to "be like, become like". We may note in passing the difference between "doing like" (imitation) and "being like" (identification; cinema actors can be wonderful impersonators of transsexuals without actually being transsexual [*cf.* the films *My Life in Pink* and *Boys Don't Cry*]).

Before this phase, a whole series of unconscious identifications have been set up, and in particular the introjections and projections described by Freud and Melanie Klein; here, however, there is a double difference, which is of some importance. According to Freud, the ego is built up by introjecting what is felt to be good and by expelling what is experienced as bad; this goes on until the child is able to feel that there are bad aspects in the ego, too. This is the point at which a representation of ego-boundaries begins to take shape. For Melanie Klein introjection and projection of good and bad elements begins straightaway, but she speaks of drive-related impulses, not of representations. As we now know, babies are able to imitate very early on in their extra-uterine life movements such as opening and closing the mouth or the eyes, sticking out the tongue, etc. Babies are in intimate contact with their parents and in particular with their mother; they can feel their parents' emotions, taking them in if they are experienced as good and shutting them out if they are experienced as bad. Babies can also attribute their own reactions to their parents; a baby who feels bad might experience his or her parents as bad. Babies need to feel comfortable and have pleasant emotions if they are to build up their narcissism and a happy experience of ongoing being.

Babies experience these emotions with their bodies, and, therefore, differently according to whether they are boy or girl. A baby does not yet realize that there are "boys" and "girls" (when he or she discovers this, it will be a traumatic experience and one that will have to be overcome); but greater muscular tonicity and penile erections are present in boys, while girls have a more diffuse experience of their body. Even without realizing it, parents may encourage or discourage their infant's bodily experiences. When the realization that there are other human beings who do not have the same body comes about, the child will have learned to appreciate— or not—what he or she is even before being able to put words to it.

The interactions between parents and their very young children who reject their assigned sex, together with what the parents have said during a series of consultations, suggest that some aspects of these interactions could well lead to gender identity disorder; this does not, of course, exclude the possibility that biological factors as yet to be discovered might also play a part. It is a well-known fact that very feminine boys were often very good-looking babies, and that passers-by would say, "What a lovely little girl you have there!", and that very masculine girls were little horrors, unattractive and restless as babies (Fridell, Zucker, Bradley, & Maing, 1996; Zucker, Wild, Bradley, & Mowry, 1993). This is a purely phenotypic factor, but it does give rise to strong interactive patterns based on social stereotypes.

Transsexualism remains an enigma. I still do not know what it is that gives rise to the repulsion transsexuals feel for their body, nor even whether the decisive factor is disgust at one's own body or the appeal of possessing that of the opposite sex.

I do have the impression that what has gradually built up in the individuals concerned is the belief that they cannot possibly live with their body as it stands, and that that firm belief has its origins in their interpretation of the conscious and unconscious messages coming from their immediate circle in general and, more specifically, from their parents or parental substitutes (there would appear to be, in this group, an inordinate number of adopted children and children brought up by one or the other of their grandmothers).

Although I would not entirely subscribe to Stoller's thesis of the boy imprinted with the feminine identity of his mother in a very close, blissful symbiosis, I do feel very much in touch with his method: the in-depth exploration of the relationship between child and parents.

The very feminine boy who refuses to be a boy is not identified with his mother, but with an ideal model constructed in part as a defensive reaction against her. Stoller spoke of a-conflictual identification with the mother. In young boys who reject their assigned sex, our study has highlighted the fact that, as soon as they are able to draw, to speak, and to play, two feminine images emerge. One is idealized: long blonde hair, a long swirling dress; while the actual mother has dark, close-cropped hair and wears jeans. The other image is that of a dangerous woman dressed in black, wearing high-heeled shoes. The real mother is neither the one nor the other: such boys do not want to be like their mother but like an idealized woman able to prevail over the dangerous aspects of their mother, whose embrace is, by turns, tender and stifling.

Thus, it became clear that, in every case, identification is necessarily identification with an ideal constructed model that, on the one hand, may borrow some aspects of the real father and mother, if they lend themselves to such a procedure, or, on the other, be quite at odds with them. Similar borrowings might involve other people, in particular those who play a significant role in the cultural ethos of the child in question.

That helped me to understand how the woman whom I mentioned earlier could say that her husband was a "constructed man" who gave her every satisfaction, even though he did not possess a penis.

So, there we have it: a psychoanalyst can see a man in someone who, initially, had a woman's body, someone who does not have a penis, yet someone with whom, in conversation, that psychoanalyst constantly has the impression of being with a man.

Paraplegics and the intersex can also feel themselves to be—and be felt as being—men. With their children, conceived thanks to artificial insemination by donor, they behave in a paternal, not maternal, manner; if they succeed in accepting their somewhat particular condition, they can turn out to be good fathers.

It is for this reason, in addition to my own experience, which goes beyond any preconceptions, that I cannot agree with some of Argentieri's conclusions on what lies ahead for patients who have undergone surgery. It can happen that some become visibly psychotic; this could lead us to believe that *the transsexual solution is a defence against psychosis*. Very few patients regret having had the operation; those who, like Quinodoz's patient, seek the help of a psychoanalyst, say that they could not have managed without surgery. Some go on to build for themselves a life in which they can find happiness.

## Conclusion

### Transsexuals

It must, all the same, be said that a hormono–surgical sex change is not a trivial matter; it is a mutilating operation which carries with it risks and possible complications. Doctors who continue to prescribe it with no venal motivation do so because they know it can help some patients, those for whom there is no other palliative treatment and certainly no other therapeutic care available.

What can psychoanalysis do? In the first place, the patient would have to agree to such a proposal, and that is a rare occurrence. We then have to face up to the fact that the way things are organized in his or her mind is hardly a good preparation for analysis. None the less, some patients have had psychoanalytic psychotherapy; they have taught me that they can be helped and supported, but that we cannot change their gender identity or their determination to "change their sex". In the USA, Lothstein has come to the same conclusion. The help we can offer will be all the more effective if we manage to remain neutral with regard to their project and not be overwhelmed by dread. Interactions in early childhood play a decisive role, and we have to accept the fact that there are some things from that distant past which just cannot be repaired. There is a psychological bedrock just as much as there is a biological one.

On the other hand, with children, as long as we work with the child *and* his or her parents, we quite often succeed in getting them to accept the sex in which they were born. Di Ceglie (Chapter Three) will in all probability agree with that view.

It is also the case with some adolescents.

### The transgenders

I have not, hitherto, mentioned transgenderism, although it forms part of the title of Argentieri's chapter, because I have no clinical experience of such people. They do not ask for psychotherapy, because they campaign for the "de-psychiatrizing" of the issue. They are outraged at the idea that anyone could think of their experience as a psychological disorder. They welcome in their midst those transsexuals who ask for hormono–surgical transformation, but consider them to be too timorous since they quietly wait for a doctor's opinion. Transgender people want the hormono–surgical procedure to become as ordinary as tattooing or piercing, and go as far as to claim that a person should be able to declare him- or herself as a man or a woman without having surgery. That would indeed dispense with a significant mutilation, as Argentieri mentions, but could society attach the label "woman" to a person who has a penis and is able to father children as a man would? Or vice-versa? That would be something of a mess, to put it mildly. No matter. The artificial uterus will tidy everything up, men and women will be equals as regards procreation, and there will no longer be "fathers" and "mothers". Gender identity is a private feeling, and society should not meddle with it. In a recent television programme on the Arte channel, Marcela Iacub said that one ought to be able to be a man in the morning and a woman at midday if that was the way the person wanted it to be. One's sex should no longer be mentioned on civil status documents. Being transgender implies the disappearance of gender, just as gender meant the disappearance of sex. There only remains *queer* identity, in which the individual is neither one gender nor the other, or perhaps both at the same time.

Militant campaigners lump together "homo" and "trans". Since homophobia is illegal, transphobia should be likened to homophobia and be made illegal too. With queer identity, homosexuality is no longer a problem. Since there are no "men" or "women" any more, there can be no persecuted homosexuality nor hated heterosexuality: all that remains is sexuality. And bi-homo parenthood (being legally the child of two men or two women)? No problem, there are no "fathers" nor "mothers" any more, just "parents".

And so goodbye to the difference between the sexes and between generations, the "sexual compass" of psychoanalysts. As they cling to their sexual compass, psychoanalysts are henceforth much more than behind the times (but we have to hang on . . .); they are so outdated that even carbon-dating would be of no use . . .

## Note

1.    Translated from the French by David Alcorn

## References

Freud, S. (1921c). Group Psychology and the Analysis of the Ego, *S.E.*, *18*: 67–143. London: Hogarth.

Fridell, S. R., Zucker, K. J., Bradley, S. J., & Maing, D. M. (1996). Physical attractiveness of girls with gender identity disorder. *Archives of Sexual Behavior*, 25(1): 17–31.

Quinodoz, D. (1998). "A fe/male transsexual patient in psychoanalysis. *International Journal of Psychoanalysis*, 79(1): 95–111.

Quinodoz. D. (2002). Termination of a fe/male transsexual patient's analysis: an example of general validity. *International Journal of Psychoanalysis*, 83: 783–798.

Rajon, A.-M. (1998). La naissance de l'identité dans le cas des ambiguïtés sexuelles. *La Psychiatrie de l'enfant*, 41(1): 5–35.

Stoller, R. (1985). *Presentations of Gender*. New Haven, CT: Yale University Press.

Zucker, K. J., Wild, J., Bradley, S. J., & Mowry, C. B. (1993), Physical attractiveness of boys with gender identity disorder, *Archives of Sexual Behavior*, 22(1): 23–36.

## Bibliography

Atlan, H. (2005). *L'utérus artificiel*. Paris: Seuil.

Califia, P. (1997). *Sex Changes: the Politics of Transgenderism*. San Francisco, CA: Cleis.

Chiland, C. (1997). *Changer de sexe*. Paris: Odile Jacob. English edition: *Transsexualism: Illusion and Reality*. P. Slotkin (Trans.). London: Continuum, 2003.

Chiland, C. (1999). *Le sexe mène le monde*. Paris: Calmann-Lévy. English edition: *Sex Makes the World Go Round*. D. Alcorn (Trans.). London: Karnac, 2008.

Chiland, C. (2003). *Le transsexualisme*, Paris: PUF. English edition: *Exploring Transsexualism*. D. Alcorn (Trans.). London: Karnac, 2005.

# CHAPTER THREE

# Between Scylla and Charybdis: exploring atypical gender identity development in children and adolescents

*Domenico Di Ceglie*

I begin with a passage from Homer's *Odyssey*, describing Ulysses' voyage home:

> Ulysses' next danger lay in passing between two cliffs, one of which harboured Scylla and the other Charybdis, her fellow-monster. Charybdis ... was a voracious woman, who had been hurled by Zeus's thunderbolt into the sea and now, thrice daily, sucked in a huge volume of water and presently spewed it out again. Scylla ... had been changed into a dog-like monster with six fearful heads and twelve feet. She would seize sailors, crack their bones, and slowly swallow them. [Graves, 1981, p. 361]

Ulysses is aware of these two dangers and instructs his crew:

> You, helmsman, here's your order—burn it in your mind—the steering-oar of our rolling ship is in your hands. Keep her clear of that smoke and surging breakers, head for those crags or she'll catch you off guard, she'll yaw over there—you'll plunge us all in ruin!

Ulysses does not mention Scylla, fearing the crew would panic, abandon their oars, and stop rowing. The ship passes through, but

Scylla manages to snatch six men from the boat whom Ulysses considered the most valiant of the crew.

This story provides us with a fitting metaphor for the dangers involved in work with children and adolescents with atypical gender identity development, children who perceive their gender identity to be in disharmony with the external reality of their body. The story of Scylla and Charybdis also offers us, I think, an approach to dealing with these dangers as well as the potential costs.

In our attempts to understand the nature of atypical gender identity development, the danger is that we are seized by the Scylla of focusing on the workings of the mind and neglecting the reality of the body, or, alternatively, we are sucked into the Charybdis of a focus on the reality of the body which neglects the contribution of the mind. The notion of the body includes here the structure and functions of the brain, as described by the neurosciences, with the limitation that biology might impose on psychic change. The challenge is to find the middle course, avoiding the risk of falling foul of either of these two polarities. However, if one takes this course in order to have a good chance of progress in our understanding of atypical gender identity development, the room for manoeuvre is limited and the possibility of straying from a safe passage is high. Ulysses does not inform his crew of both dangers for fear that they would get too close to Charybdis, whom he considers the greatest danger for all of them, with the consequence that six sailors are seized by Scylla. This suggests that there is a cost to be paid for the survival of the whole crew. Intriguingly, we are told it is the most valiant members of the crew who are seized by Scylla. Are the heroic activities of these crew members responsible for exposing them to Scylla? In other words, was their downfall a consequence of their heroic valiance? Or were they foolish in colluding with Ulysses' turning a blind eye to the dangers of Scylla?

The story provides a warning of the risk that crusaders of one kind or another may run in the field of atypical gender identity development.

I use the term crusader to represent a state of mind characterized by a firm belief in a particular goal and a great level of persistence in achieving it. In this state of mind, "giving up" or postponing the achievement is not an option.

There is a risk for the professional involved in this area of work of becoming "a crusader", by taking a very definite view or set of beliefs about aetiology and treatment and then pursuing a course of action at all costs, disregarding the consequences of such action. This state of mind in a professional, although partly due to personality characteristics, is often also the result of a process of re-enactment of the mental states of children and adolescents with gender identity disorders. Britton (1981) describes in detail this particular type of interaction between patient and professional in his paper "Re-enactment as an unwitting professional response to family dynamics".

Within this perspective, I would like to compare here Ulysses' state of mind with that of Oedipus's, as highlighted by Bion (1967) in his paper "On arrogance". These two mythological characters can represent two different stances in facing a particular reality. Bion writes,

> I shall rehearse the Oedipus myth from a point of view which makes the sexual crime a peripheral element of a story in which the central crime is the arrogance of Oedipus in vowing to lay bare the truth at no matter what cost. [*ibid.*]

Like a crusader, the pursuit of an objective, at no matter what cost, is a significant danger in all our work, but particularly in the field of gender identity development, where the pressures are such that one can be tempted to resort to a rigid and inflexible position. An example of this is the belief that children would adapt at a very young age to whatever gender they were assigned by parents and then consistently reared in that gender. This assumption led to a mistake of rearing a biological boy, whose penis had been damaged by a botched circumcision, as a girl. At an early age, this child was operated on, his penis and testicles removed, and an opening mimicking a vagina was constructed. This child, as an adult, reverted to a male biological sex and, tragically, eventually killed himself. The story is described in detail in the book *As Nature Made Him* (Colapinto, 2000). As a reaction to this case, some authors have taken the strongly opposite view that it is only the brain, with its structure and functions, which determines our gender identity and that psycho-social influences play no role. Taking this stance will obviously affect the management of people with atypical gender identity disorder.

Facing the twin dangers of Scylla and Charybdis, Ulysses, by contrast with Bion's Oedipus, seemed to have taken account of the potential costs involved in his approach to the treacherous passage. He had made an assessment of risk and acted accordingly. His stance is more flexible and, therefore, negotiation is possible. Bearing in mind this perspective on the metaphor, I shall now examine the phenomenology of gender identity disorders and some of the basic research findings and then discuss how this links to therapeutic work.

The features of an atypical gender identity development in children and adolescents have been clearly described in the *DSM IV* (see Table 1) and *ICD10* classifications, and under the diagnostic category of gender identity disorder.

There is currently a debate among professionals and users' groups on whether or not this diagnostic category should be retained. I will not go into the arguments which have been put forward on both sides. However, the existence of well-defined diagnostic criteria has enabled a limited number of follow-up studies to ascertain the outcome in adulthood of children and adolescents who describe these experiences and show these types of behaviours. Zucker (1985) has collated all the long-term follow-up studies of children with gender identity difficulties referred to mental health professionals as shown in Table 2.

Green (1987) followed up forty-four boys with atypical gender identity development and found that thirty-three were classified as homosexual or bisexual in terms of phantasy. Out of thirty boys who had had overt sexual experiences, twenty-four were classified as bisexual or homosexual, and six were classified as heterosexual. It would also appear that many of the boys who classified themselves as "bisexual" in adolescence moved to a more exclusively homosexual orientation in adulthood.

We are currently undertaking a follow-up study of children with gender identity disorder (GID) who are now beyond the age of eighteen, and the initial data show comparable outcomes to previous studies. It is clear from these follow-up studies that, for the majority of children, the experience of an atypical gender identity is transient, while for a minority it persists throughout adolescence

*Table 1.*

---

A.  A strong and persistent cross-gender identification (not merely a desire for any perceived cultural advantages of being the other sex). In children the disturbance is manifested by four (or more) of the following.
1.  Repeatedly stated desire to be, or insistence that he/she is the other sex.
2.  In boys, preference for cross-dressing or simulating female attire; in girls, insistence on only wearing stereotypical masculine clothing.
3.  Strong and persistent preferences for cross-sex roles in make-believe play or persistent fantasies of being the other sex.
4.  Intense desire to participate in the stereotypical games and pastimes of the other sex.
5.  Strong preference for playmates of the other sex. In adolescent and adults, the disturbance is manifested in symptoms such as stated desire to be the other sex, frequent passing as the other sex, desire to live and be treated as the other sex, or the conviction that he/she has the typical feelings and reactions of the other sex.
B.  Persistent discomfort with his/her sex or sense of inappropriateness in the gender role of the sex.
    In children, the disturbance is manifested by any of the following: in boys, the assertion that his penis and testes are disgusting or will disappear, or assertion that it would be better not to have a penis, or aversion towards rough and tumble play and rejection of male stereotypical toys, games and activities;
    in girls, the rejection of urinating in a sitting position, assertion that she has or will grow a penis, or assertion that she does not want to grow breasts or menstruate, or marked aversion toward normative female clothing.
    In adolescents and adults, the disturbance is manifested by symptoms such as preoccupation with getting rid of primary and secondary sex characteristics (e.g., request for hormones, surgery, or other procedures to physically alter sexual characteristics to stimulate the other other sex), or belief that he/she was born the wrong sex.
C.  The disturbance is not concurrent with a physical intersex condition.

---

until adulthood. More than half of the children with GID develop a gay identity.

However, at present, it is not possible to predict from early childhood with any certainty the future outcome of the gender identity development. It is not clear what the connection is between the experience of an atypical gender identity development and a gay identity in adolescence or in adulthood.

*Table 2.* Long term follow-up studies of children with gender identity disorders (from Zucker, 1985).

| Outcome | No. of cases | % of total cases |
| --- | --- | --- |
| Transsexual | 5 | 5.3 |
| Homosexual or bisexual | 43 | 45.7 |
| Transvestite(heterosexual) | 1 | 1.1 |
| Heterosexual | 21 | 22.3 |
| Uncertain | 24 | 25.5 |
| Total | 94 | 100 |

In 1964, Stoller proposed the concept of core gender identity. He saw this as:

> produced by the infant–parent relationship, the child's perception of its external genitalia, and a biologic force, which results from the biologic variables of sex (chromosomes, gonads, hormones, internal accessory reproductive structures and external genitalia). [p. 453]

Stoller believed that the core gender identity is established before the fully developed phallic stage, although gender identity continues to develop into adolescence or beyond (1964, p. 453). He further stated that the beliefs comprising the "mental structure" of the core gender identity are the earliest part of gender identity to develop and are relatively permanent after the child reaches four or five years of age (Stoller, 1992).

The above research data and clinical experience show that there may be more flexibility in gender identity development than Stoller's concept of core gender identity would imply. Only in some children and adolescents with an atypical development does the core gender identity have the structural characteristics described by Stoller. In 1998, I proposed the concept of atypical gender identity organization (AGIO) as a clinical entity that can be examined under a number of parameters relevant to clinical management, which are described in a paper, "Reflections on the nature of the "atypical gender identity organization" (Di Ceglie, 1998a). These are as follows:

1. *Rigidity–flexibility.* This refers to the capacity of the organization to remain unchangeable, or, alternatively, to be amenable

to evolution in the course of development. Only in particular cases will it possess the unchangeable structural qualities of Stoller's core gender identity.

2.  *Timing of the AGIO formation.* Atypical organizations that develop very early in the child's life seem more likely to become rigidly structured than organizations that develop later.

3.  *Identifiable traumatic events in the child's life in relationship to the AGIO formation. In some cases the AGIO is formed as a psychological coping strategy in relation to a traumatic event in childhood.* The earlier the trauma occurs, the more likely it is that the organization will acquire rigid and unchangeable qualities. Perry, Pollard, Blakley, Baker, and Vigilante (1995), in a paper on childhood trauma, suggested that during a critical period in the development of the brain, mental states, such as hyperarousal or dissociative states, which are coping mechanisms, organize neural systems, thus leading to the creation of traits. One can hypothesize that if the response to traumatic experience has led to the formation of an AGIO in early childhood, this can become an established trait which is less amenable to change.

4.  *Where the formation of the AGIO can be located on the continuum from the paranoid–schizoid to the depressive position.* The hypothesis here is that if the AGIO is formed within a mental functioning dominated by paranoid–schizoid processes in response to a traumatic event, it is more likely to become very structured and therefore not amenable to change. Alternatively, if it is formed within a mental functioning of the depressive position, it is likely that the organization will be amenable to evolution.

Biological factors can also contribute to the development of the atypical gender identity organisation. Hormonal influences on the brain during critical periods of development have been suggested (Kruijver, 2004). A difference has been identified in "the bed nucleus of the stria terminalis" of the brain between male-to-female transsexuals and non-transsexual males (Kruijver et al., 2000; Zhou, Hofman, Gooren, & Swaab, 1995). However, the sample was small and the data needs replication.

The implications of these differences in terms of changes in specific psychological functions are unclear. It is not known whether these differences in the brain may contribute to the persistence of the atypical gender identity organization in some people.

Whatever the factors involved in the formation of the atypical gender identity organization, therapeutic explorations over a long period of time will clarify the characteristics of the organization and therefore guide therapeutic management.

Britton, in his book *Beliefs and Imagination* (1998), makes a distinction between beliefs and phantasies. He states,

> Beliefs have consequences: they arouse feelings influence perceptions and promote actions . . . Phantasies, conscious or unconscious, which are not the object of belief, do not have consequences: disavowal therefore can be used to evade these consequences. [p. 11]

A therapeutic exploration can help to differentiate between these two states of mind as part of the atypical gender identity organization, leading to an understanding of the substantial different expectations by the individual concerned; that is to say, the expectation that the body will need to be changed *vs.* the possibility of entertaining other identities in phantasy. The following interaction during a family session illustrates this point. The interaction involves a thirteen-year-old teenager with a well-established atypical gender identity, a biological female who has the self-perception of being a boy, her/his mother, stepfather, and two therapists.

| | |
|---|---|
| Female therapist (FT): | What would you like to be called? |
| Max: | Now? It's certainly not Sarah. |
| FT: | What would you like us to call you? |
| Max: | I don't know. |
| Mother (M): | We just call Max, Max. But when I hear somebody else calling her, Sarah, or something, I just . . . |
| Max: | Why do you say "her"? |
| M: | Sorry, sorry. |
| Father: | That's the hardest bit . . . |
| M: | It's the "he" and the "she" because it's really difficult and I feel weird calling Max "her" or "she". Yeah. (To Max) I feel weird calling you it. |
| FT: | Is that the bit that hurts the most? |

| | |
|---|---|
| Max: | Yes. (M) says it all the time. |
| M: | I do. I do. Yeah. |
| FT: | But do you feel (hurt) with your mother or with everyone? |
| Max: | No, [Male therapist] calls me it too. |
| FT: | Does it hurt the same? |
| Max: | Yes. |
| FT: | It hurts the same. |
| Max: | Yes. |
| M: | I know you'd rather be called "he" but I do try, promise, we both do. |
| Male therapist (MT): | But I think it is a difficult issue to tackle because it's a bit similar to an English boy, born in England, brought up in England, about fifteen, sixteen, who emigrates to France and then goes around and says to everybody that I'm French. That I want to be considered French. While his accent will show that he is not French. So this is . . . |
| Max: | No, that's not it though, because he wants to be, he isn't, but I am. |
| MT: | But that is one of the problems because, of course, what your body says is different from what you feel inside you are. Like in this person, what he would like to be is French and this is different from what his accent, at least, you know, no other features . . . |
| Max: | I don't want to be, I don't like to be . . . a boy. |
| FT: | You are a boy. |
| Max: | Yes. |

An extract from another session shows the strength of the conviction of this teenager and the difficulties in tolerating uncertainty or that the mother could have another point of view.

> M:    Max has asked us specifically on several occasions not to call him Sarah because we have called him Max since he was incy, and to say "he" and not "she". And he's explained that it really, really hurts when someone says "she". And also it's ever so complicated if I introduce him as "she" because people think I've gone mad so . . .

Max:    You sound as if you're just doing it . . .

M:      Because you've asked me to . . ..

Max:    Yeah, one of the reasons. Why aren't you doing it for you?

M:      Also for me, because eventually if you do go ahead and have all the treatment I'm gonna have . . .

Max:    Why do you say "if"?

M:      Well, all right then, "when". I'm gonna look pretty stupid if I'm the only person on the planet calling you "she".

Max:    You sound as if you're just worried about what you do.

M:      No, it's for you and for everybody. What you need to understand is that it takes some time for somebody like me to readjust and I do try, really, really, hard because the last thing I want is to upset you . . .

MT:     The important point that you are making is that you feel that there should be no doubt about who you are . . .

Max:    Yeah.

MT:     . . . in this case you feel that you are a boy and there should be no doubt that you are a boy. And when you pick up any doubt about it, or that people are uncertain about it, that's very upsetting for you . . .

Max continued during the course of his treatment with us to remain fixed in his beliefs that he was a boy and never shifted from this position. At the age of eighteen he was referred to an adult gender identity service for further management and, as far as we know, now lives as a man. This interaction shows the determination of this teenager in achieving his goal and the difficulty of the mother in not being able to steer a safe passage between two perspectives but having to strictly adhere only to one.

Another case shows a quite different outcome.

Kevin was referred to the gender identity development service at the age of fifteen as he presented with a gender identity disorder associated with a number of borderline features. He was convinced he was a girl and wished to live in a female role, although the intensity of his conviction tended to fluctuate. He had a particularly close relationship to his mother and any separation from her would lead to the development of minor physical or psychological symptoms requiring frequent visits to his general practitioner. He had a very poor self image and his sense of identity would fluctuate. At one time, for instance, two years prior to his referral to us, he developed an intense wish to convert to Catholicism and acquire a Catholic identity. During this time he became totally absorbed in learning about the history of saints, religious rules and rituals, and attended the local parish regularly to receive instructions in preparation to become a member of the Catholic community. While preoccupied with religion, his gender identity problems seemed to become less intense or disappear. In the year prior to the referral he had attempted suicide through an overdose of Paracetamol following a perceived rejection by his parents. He had periods of intense despair, and at times would feel empty. He had been in therapy during his childhood with a male therapist and then, in the previous three years, with a female therapist. His gender identity issues, which included at times cross-dressing and wearing make up, had clearly emerged in the course of his therapy. However, they had largely remained a secret restricted to his parents and extended family. It was reported that at school he was very isolated from friends, and would spend the lunchtime hour hidden in a cupboard. From the referral of the therapist, who was bringing this therapy to an end as she had to leave her job, it appears that the parents had strongly supported his psychotherapy as they expected that it would change their son and make him acceptable to them. There was a feeling that they found it difficult to accept and love Kevin as he was.

Kevin had been referred to the gender identity development clinic with an intention that he would continue in individual therapy, perhaps with an increased frequency, given the seriousness of his difficulties. In discussing this referral, we felt that previous interventions had perhaps unwittingly gone along with the powerful parental projection into the professionals that Kevin should change before he could be accepted and loved, and that meanwhile the parents could see hardly anything positive in him. Kevin seemed frequently to perceive his therapist as critical and persecutory, while his therapist felt exasperated, as he presented himself as extremely resistant to change. We felt that, at this stage of his development, it was best to have family therapy sessions and resist pressures, particularly from his parents, for further individual work. The aims of the therapy would be to allow open communication so that the parents could become aware of his gender identity issues, the fact that he was unhappy about his body as a boy, his wish to cross-dress, and to reduce the intense sense of catastrophe and shame with which these feelings and wishes were associated in Kevin. It was also important for the parents to become aware of their unrealistic expectation, leading to the offer of conditional love and acceptance of Kevin as a person.

A colleague and I therefore saw the family for family sessions for about one year. During this time the family became able to explore more openly Kevin's gender identity issues and to recognize his relationship difficulties and the impact that this was having on the whole family, including two younger siblings. The father, who had hardly been in contact with the previous services, attended the sessions regularly and became more involved and interested in his son. We also constructed a family tree as a way of exploring relationships within the extended family and to encourage Kevin's curiosity about his background. The absence of curiosity seemed to be a major feature in the family's interaction with us; they were more interested in talking about factual events and giving a rundown of their weekly routine. This, at times, had a paralysing effect on the therapists, who had to work hard to maintain interest and curiosity in making links. In the course of the sessions, it emerged that in the past Kevin would lock himself in cupboards in school at lunchtime in order not to be seen. We drew attention to the fact that Kevin, while in the corridors on the way to the consulting rooms, moved in a strange and awkward way. He walked hunched up and looking at the floor, a gait which was suggestive of a neurological condition. There was no evidence that there was a physical cause for his gait. When we explored this in the sessions, Kevin eventually was able to say that he walked in that strange way as he did not want to be seen. It became clear that his way of moving and his locking himself in cupboards had the same meaning: hiding himself. In his way of walking he was not able to see, and he projected this experience on to other people with the resulting perception that other people would not see him. We were aware of his profound sense of shame for not feeling right in his body, so that his attempts to become invisible were a way of dealing with this. Paradoxically, quite the opposite occurred, as he made himself even more visible and an object of curiosity to other people.

Through this work, a shift seemed to occur which enabled the parents to be more understanding of Kevin and more able to accept him as he is. When it felt appropriate, and with the family's consent, we contacted the school to help the staff to have a better understanding of Kevin's difficulties so that they could devise a strategy to support him within the school context. In the family therapy the issue of individual therapy re-emerged, but we felt it was important that this was arranged at Kevin's request and should be a separate space for him to explore feelings in privacy. Quite some time was spent with the family exploring the difference between privacy and secrecy, and that therapy would provide a private space for him. His secretive attitude in the past had been another way of dealing with the shame about his unwanted feelings about his gender. Kevin was seen in individual therapy once a week while we continued to see the family at monthly intervals and liaise with his college. He was also seen by our paediatric endocrinologist to discuss his concerns about his body. The creation of this therapeutic framework proved to be containing and the suicidal risk lessened. He became more aware of his needs, and could talk more openly in the family sessions. Psychoanalytically orientated family work paved the way to a more productive engagement in individual work. By the end of his contact with us at the age of eighteen, Kevin's beliefs that he was a girl in a male body seemed to have shifted, and although he was not feeling comfortable with being a boy, he did not wish to pursue any treatment aimed at changing his body. He left college with some qualifications and found voluntary work in a charity. This outcome could not have been easily predicted from the outset and only long term therapeutic work enabled him to clarify his gender identity and to decide what was best for him in the long term.

As the causation of the atypical gender identity organization is unclear, and probably the result of a complex interaction of many factors during development, at our Service we have developed a model of management in which altering the gender identity disorder *per se* is not a primary therapeutic objective. Our primary therapeutic concern is the developmental processes that, in our clinical and research experience, seem most often to have been negatively affected in the child (Table 3).

While changing the gender identity disorder itself is not the primary aim, it is possible that, by targeting and improving the developmental processes that may underpin gender development, it will be affected in a secondary way and will not lead to establishment of an atypical gender identity in adulthood. The aims outlined in Table 3 can be achieved through various psychotherapeutic interventions, ranging from individual to family and group therapy. Social and educational interventions are also useful. It is important that these are well co-ordinated and integrated in a comprehensive management plan.

Certain aims are more relevant in some cases than in others. A detailed account of the therapeutic aims is given in a previous paper "Management and therapeutic aims with children and adolescents with gender identity disorder and their families", Di Ceglie (1998b).

The recognition and non-judgemental acceptance of the gender identity problem, which is not the result of the child's conscious choice, is important. Without this, the child would experience feelings of rejection, psychological splitting processes would increase to cope with this, and no further therapeutic work could be under-

*Table 3.*  Primary therapeutic aims (from Di Ceglie, 1998a).

1.  To foster recognition and non-judgemental acceptance of gender identity problems.
2.  To ameliorate associated behavioural, emotional and relationship difficulties (Coates & Spector Person, 1985).
3.  To break the cycle of secrecy.
4.  To activate interest and curiosity by exploring the impediments to them.
5.  To encourage exploration of the mind–body relationship by promoting close collaboration among professionals in different specialities, including a paediatric endocrinologist.
6.  To allow mourning processes to occur (Bleiberg et al., 1986).
7.  To enable symbol formation and symbolic thinking (Segal, 1957).
8.  To promote separation and differentiation.
9.  To enable the child or adolescent and the family to tolerate uncertainty in gender identity development.
10. To sustain hope.

taken. Group work for parents of children with gender identity disorders can be very helpful in this respect, as it helps the parents to realize that their problem is not unique (Di Ceglie & Coates-Thümmel, 2005).

Where an inability to mourn attachment figures has interfered with gender identity development, work enabling mourning to occur may secondarily alter an atypical gender identity development.

The following case vignette illustrates this point.

James was referred to the Gender Identity Development Service at the age of eight years. At the assessment interviews, he said that, since the age of four or five years, he had very much wished he were a girl. He had been secretly dressing up in his mother's clothes. He liked to play with dolls and cuddly toys and fantasized that he was a mother feeding them. He played weddings where he liked to be the bride. At school he wanted to play with girls and avoided rough-and-tumble play or other activities with boys.

His maternal grandmother had looked after him from the age of six months to five years, as his mother was often away working. The grandmother involved him in many activities, including cooking and tidying up the house. After her sudden death in hospital, James developed a gender identity disorder. He could not talk about the loss of his grandmother, or even mention her, but he concretely identified with her and persistently wished to continue with all the activities in exactly the same way as he had done with her. Family therapy, focusing on a family tree constructed over many sessions, enabled the narrative of his experiences with his grandmother to be developed. The clinical features of his gender identity disorder gradually reduced in intensity and disappeared.

In this case the psychological work focused not only on mourning processes, but it also removed the secrecy about his gender problem, encouraged curiosity about its origins, and established a link between his atypical gender development and the way he had coped with the loss of his grandmother. Symbol formation was stimulated, so that he could have a mental picture of her and memories of the past, rather than concretely identifying with and becoming her. Increased contact with his father seemed also to play an important role.

## Conclusion

Ulysses' progress through Scylla and Charybdis was made possible by forward thinking and a clear strategy. This included the definition of a path to follow and instruction to his sailors on how to approach this passage. The therapist's awareness of having clear therapeutic aims provides a pathway to enable the child's progress in the development of gender identity. It avoids the danger that the therapist and child become trapped in a polarization between the mind and body, which would impede exploration and progress.

Our work with children and adolescents aims to expand their creative capacity and remove the feelings of shame and stigma which are often associated to the experience of diversity. We are complex creatures. The understanding and non-judgemental acceptance of atypical gender identity development make richer the world we inhabit.

## References

American Psychiatric Association (1994). *Diagnostic and Statistical Manual of Mental Disorders (DSM-IV)* (4th edn). Washington, DC: APA.

Bion, W. R. (1967). On arrogance. In: *Second Thoughts*. New York: Jason Aronson.

Britton, R. (1981). Re-enactment as an unwitting professional response to family dynamics. In: S. Box, B. Copley, J. Magagna, & E. Moustaki (Eds.), *Psychotherapy With Families: An Analytic Approach* (pp.48–59). London: Routledge & Kegan Paul.

Britton, R. (1998). *Beliefs and Imagination*. London: Routledge.

Colapinto, J. (2000). *As Nature Made Him*. London: Quartet Books Ltd.

Di Ceglie, D. (1998a). Reflections on the nature of the "atypical gender identity organization". In: D. Di Ceglie & D. Freedman (Eds.), *A Stranger in My Own Body: Atypical Gender Identity Development and Mental Health* (pp. 9–25). London: Karnac.

Di Ceglie, D. (1998b). Management and therapeutic aims with children and adolescents with gender identity disorder and their families. In: D. Di Ceglie & D. Freedman (Eds.), *A Stranger in My Own Body Atypical Gender Identity Development and Mental Health* (pp. 185–197). London: Karnac.

Di Ceglie, D., & Coates-Thümmel, E. (2005). An experience of group work with parents of children and adolescents with gender identity disorder. In: *Clinical Child Psychology and Psychiatry* (pp. 387–396). London; Thousand Oaks, CA; New Delhi: Sage.

Graves, R. (1981). *The Greek Myths*, Vol. 2. London: Penguin.

Green, R. (1987). *The "Sissy Boy Syndrome" and the Development of Homosexuality*. New Haven, CT: Yale University Press.

Kruijver, F. P. M. (2004). Sex in the brain. Gender differences in the human hypothalamus and adjacent areas. Relationship transsexualism, sexual orientation, sex hormone receptors and endocrine status. Doctoral Thesis, University of Amsterdam, Print: Ponsen and Looijen BV.

Kruijver, F. P. M., Zhou, J.-N., Pool, C. W., Hofman, M. A., Gooren, L. J. G., & Swaab, D. F. (2000). Male to female transsexuals have female neuron numbers in a limbic nucleus. *Journal of Clinical Endocrinology and Metabolism, 85*(5): 2034–2041.

Perry, B. D., Pollard, R. A., Blakley, T. L., Baker, W. L., & Vigilante, D. (1995). Childhood trauma, the neurobiology of adaptation, and use-dependent development of the brain: how states become traits. *Infant Mental Health Journal, 16*(4): 271–291.

Stoller, R. (1964). The hermaphroditic identity of hermaphrodites. *Journal of Nervous and Mental Disease, 139*: 453–457.

Stoller, R. (1992). Gender identity development and prognosis: a summary. In: C. Chiland & J. G. Young (Eds.), *New Approaches to Mental Health from Birth to Adolescence* (pp. 78–87). New Haven, CT: Yale University Press.

Zhou, J.-N., Hofman, M. A., Gooren, L. J., & Swaab, D. F. (1995). A sex difference in the human brain and its relation to transsexuality. *Nature, 378*: 68–70.

Zucker, K. J. (1985). Cross-gender identified children. In: B. Steiner (Ed.), *Gender Dysphoria* (pp. 75–174). New York: Plenum Press.

# CHAPTER FOUR

# Atypical gender identity development: on biological and psychological factors

## Discussion of Domenico Di Ceglie's paper

*Eulàlia Torras de Beà*

My experience with children and teenagers with gender identity disorders comes from my work in a Mental Health Service for Children and Teenagers with every kind of psychopathology (Centres de Salut Mental Infantil i Juvenil [de la Fundació Eulàlia Torras de Beà], Barcelona). So, although we are referred children with atypical gender identity, our experience is limited and, for us, working with these children is not easy. I imagine that it is never easy. I do not know whether different working contexts can also create different professional perspectives and attitudes towards the problem.

Dr Di Ceglie speaks of the need to take into account both "the workings of the mind and the reality of the body". I completely agree that we have to consider these two aspects: the biological factors and the psychological–relational factors in the evolution towards the establishment of a gender identity, even of any identity, I would say.

I also agree that many biological (chromosomal, hormonal, neurological, and so on) factors are only partially known. I think that is what concerns the psychological and social factors, although their influence is indisputable in every person's evolution, in our clinical general practice (I mean outside of psychotherapeutic exploration), we can often only take into account those that seem or are "visible" or conscious, for instance, a mother's overt communication of wishing to have a boy (or a girl) instead of the child she has; a mother dressing her boy or girl in the style of the other gender, or a father with some or other characteristics, and so on.

I think that thousands of other minute, hidden, unconscious, psychological factors, relational moments, or social pressures, which can be strongly determining, escape our powers of observation. It is very difficult to gauge the actual influence of all these psychological factors, for instance the strength of the mother's cross-gender identity projections and many others, unless we have the opportunity to engage in exploration of all the participants in the family constellation, something not easy to organize or do.

On the other hand, many other boys and girls may have lived in similar atmospheres and suffered similar or worse supposed influences and projections, and they have not developed an atypical gender identity. It is the same when we talk about psychogenetic factors in homosexuality, etc.

The resulting gender identity might depend on the encounter and collusion between parent–child projections, on the one hand, and the facility for specific kinds of introjections, on the other. For instance, James, eight years old, in Dr Di Ceglie's paper, developed a pathological process of mourning and resorted to an unhealthy identification with his deceased grandmother, who had looked after him for nearly five years. For me, it is not difficult to understand the transient or definitive identification with her that he developed in the place of a normal process of mourning. However, I find it more difficult to accept the idea that her involving him in cooking and tidying could have had a prominent place in his gender identity problem. Many parents actively encourage their sons to help with domestic tasks and to be self-sufficient in this domain, without their children developing an atypical gender identity. But perhaps, combined with other aspects of his milieu, it was a factor with that particular boy.

The paper has also made me wonder what prominence we should give to the internal world and fantasy in the identification–identity issue, both to those fantasies that are acted out as atypical gender identity, and to those that remain latent in the internal reality without being acted out. I think we agree that, in order to know the personality, identifications, and identity, and, of course, the gender–sexual side of these identifications and identity, we need to explore that inner world and its fantasies. But I do not think that there is necessarily a direct relation between the quality and prevalence of the fantasies and their external expression as happens, for instance, in gender identity. On the contrary, I think that there are many nuances. Some men and women can entertain strong and frequent fantasies of, say, belonging to the other gender without being or becoming transexual or homosexual. Others seem to act out fantasies or elements of their internal world that they are not aware of and cannot express verbally.

To return to a previous point, Dr Di Ceglie tells us that, for us professionals, it could be easy to fall into the trap of focusing on only one of the two polar positions: biological factors or the workings of the mind. I am not sure that I have grasped the full import of what Dr Di Ceglie means when he speaks of this risk, which he portrays using the metaphor of Scylla and Charybdis, but, from my experience, I agree that all too frequently we professionals consider only one of the two poles.

Sometimes I have found that it is easy to talk with colleagues, psychotherapists and psychoanalysts, about the psychogenetic factors, but it is difficult to include the biological side of things. Even more, as a psychoanalyst, one is actually supposed to put all one's emphasis on the organization of the mind, disregarding biological factors or considering them only as a consequence of the former.

I remember once, in a psychoanalytical discussion group on small children (four to five years of age) with severe obsessive organizations, I said that, besides psychogenetic factors, I did not discard the possibility of biological factors in such evolutions. A colleague expressed his surprise and disagreement quite vehemently, adding that he was surprised that I, as a psychoanalyst, should consider factors outside the psychogenetic domain. It was as if, by not discarding the possibility of biological factors being involved, I was doubting or even denying, the existence of psychogenetic factors. Nobody contradicted him. I did not know whether all of them agreed with him or whether they did not dare to contradict him, like in the story of the Emperor's new clothes.

What I meant then, and I think this is similar to what may happen with atypical gender identity, is that our knowledge of genetics may still be very incomplete, but the experts know much more now than they did about many things, including chromosomes and other genetic factors.

I refer, for instance, to the effects of the transfer of minute portions of one chromosome to another, the combinations or the multiplication of these changes, the question of quality and quantity of these transfers, etc. I mean that the issue is not only one of the combination of XY or XX chromosomes, but also the quality and the quantity of tiny changes in these chromosomes.

Another important field, today, is research into the mutual biological (and perhaps psychological at some level) regulation between mother and foetus. Current research in biology (Haig, in Harvard, reported by Slavin) has revealed the biological negotiation between foetus and mother to get what both need for their own metabolisms, and the conflicts involved. The foetus, in order to get what it needs for its own development, penetrates and modifies the metabolism and physiology of the mother. The mother's physiology accommodates these changes, but when there is a conflict of needs, her body reacts by trying to regulate her own and the foetus's metabolism. This negotiation involves the metabolism of sugar, blood availability, and blood pressure, hormonal equilibrium, and hormonal phases, etc. We know that psychological factors are also involved in these modifications and evolution. Researchers suggest that, when the conflict is serious, it can lead to disorders of the constants of the mother, with severe consequences, among them diabetes or malignant hypertension.

We know that cells of the foetus loaded with all kinds of antigens circulate in the mother's blood. It is well known that the reaction of the mother's body (for instance in Rh incompatibility) can produce severe problems in the foetus, and even its death.

Today, we know about not only these serious incompatibilities but also what are called semi-incompatibilities, which produce results that are not so dramatic, but that do modify the evolution of the foetus and the mother in many ways.

It is probably not too much of an exaggeration to conjecture that mutual mental and biological influences between mother and foetus can provoke semi-incompatibilities or interferences in different areas, influencing every aspect of evolution. One of these factors could be hormones affecting the foetus's brain, according to at least one theory. All of this is intertwined with psychological–relational factors after birth.

On the other hand, theories about the influence of neurological factors—changes in groups of specific neurons or axons, etc.—remind me of the problem of dyslexia and what has been said about its causes. Each school of researchers on neurological factors invokes different neurological changes in different parts of the brain as the cause of dyslexia. Not a single one of these theories has been validated. Different schools of neurologists disagree with the findings of other schools. Moreover, all these theories contradict current knowledge in the field of neuroplasticity. Whether or not this example is relevant to the problem of gender identity, it is still worth thinking about.

A second point I want to make is about countertransference and prejudice. I think this is something Dr Di Ceglie does not speak about in his paper, where I have not found the least sign of prejudice. Maybe the reason is that working intensively with these problems helps the professional to elaborate and overcome his or her prejudices. And, on the contrary, perhaps our more general work context makes it more difficult for us to work through and overcome ours. How much prejudice would come from personal characteristics and how much from our general cultural backgrounds? I wonder whether prejudice varies with different cultures.

I would differentiate between difficulties in the countertransference and prejudice, even though they are related and, for instance, the latter can aggravate difficulties in the former. I refer not only to our response to a particular patient and his or her specific characteristics, for instance the defensive system, but also to our reaction to the problem as a whole. Sometimes it is difficult to bear the closed, rigid, rejecting attitude of some adolescents with transsexual problems. But, other times, what is difficult to tolerate and accept is the mere existence of such problems. These are factors that complicate our work with these children.

One example of the prejudice we can observe would be our aims in starting a psychotherapy with a child with atypical gender identity. Not infrequently we start with the idea—conscious or unconscious, acknowledged or not—of changing the child's gender identification. Quite often it is the result of our bowing to the wishes and the pressure—projective identification—of parents. Dr Di Ceglie illustrates this in his second clinical example.

I think we are not always aware of having this aim (our professional superego prevents us), and that, especially when it is unconscious, this aim can result in the non-feasibility or interruption of the treatment.

I agree with Dr Di Ceglie that what the psychotherapy must offer is the possibility of analytic exploration so that the child can use and develop his or her own resources. However, sometimes we find ourselves in the situation where the parents do not let the child continue if they do not feel that our main target is to change the child's gender identity, or that we are getting "results" in that direction.

To give another example, I remember one adolescent who complained about being a girl. From the beginning she told me about her rejection of her body, her suffering at home and at school when she was four or five years old because she felt different and not accepted. Later, she realized she had to hide her feelings in general because they made the others feel uncomfortable and rejecting. She undertook treatment at the age of eighteen because she did not feel good and felt anxious and alone, even though she had a lot of male and female friends with whom she had been able to talk about her condition. In the treatment, I noticed I had to choose my words because I feared hurting her if I said things the way they came to my mind. I did not know whether this situation resulted from prejudices of mine that appeared in the form of words I feared were not adequate, or from her sensitivity, because she had suffered rejection so many times. I felt I was being tested and I was disconcerted because I could not find a way of talking about it openly. I clearly colluded with her defensive system. After some months she told me that the first days she had been testing me, paying a lot of attention to every word I said. "If I had noticed that you thought of making me change, I would have felt rejected and would not have come again." She had tried a previous consultation and had not continued.

In my experience, parents consult more often for boys who want to dress like girls, play with girls, and avoid rough (or not so rough) games than for girls wanting to dress like boys, playing boyish games, etc. They seem more afraid about the evolution of sons. So, in general, I have more often seen small boys of four to six who did not say they were not boys, but showed their "conviction" or feelings through moving and playing like girls, drawing princesses with long dresses, long blonde hair and red lips, and enjoying wearing their mothers' scarves and other feminine accessories with the mannerisms of young women, to the extent that they made others confuse them with girls through their style and behaviour.

In my experience, few parents of boys and girls between about four and six with crossed-gender identification come through their own initiative. More often they come by recommendation or pressure from the school. They often only want to be reassured and to forget the whole thing.

I remember one boy of four whose mother used to dress him in pink: pink trousers and sports shoes, pink T-shirt with feminine drawings, and so on. Even his "boy" clothes seemed feminine, partially due to his way of moving. His father was also a little feminine in his movements, nothing startling, but clearly noticeable. They came for consultation at the school's suggestion because the boy only played with girls and refused to participate in boys' games and sports. Any game was too rough for him. The parents came, but were not interested in the consultation. Moreover, they felt offended and adopted a rather querulous tone, as if to demonstrate that the school was absolutely wrong and owed them an explanation. Later on they moved the boy to another school.

The few transsexual adolescents I have seen, all of them in the Public Service, accepted only a short period of psychotherapy. All of them were waiting to be eighteen so that they could undergo surgical transformation. They were crusaders.

To conclude, I agree with Dr Di Ceglie in that what we can offer to children and teenagers with problems with their gender identity is psychotherapeutic exploration to enhance their capacities, develop new resources, and adjust better to the life they finally choose to live.

## Bibliography

Chiland, C. (2003). *Le transsexualisme*. Paris: P.U.F Que sais-je?
Chiland, C. (1997). *Changer de sexe*. Paris: Ed. Odile Jacob.

Di Ceglie, D. (1995). Gender identity disorders in children and adolescents. *British Journal of Hospital Medicine, 53*: 251–256.

Di Ceglie, D. (1998a). Management and therapeutic aims with children and adolescents with gender identity disorders and their families. In: D. Di Ceglie & D. Freedman (Eds.), *A Stranger In My Own Body. Atypical Gender Identity Development and Mental Health* (pp.185–197). London: Karnac.

Di Ceglie, D. (1998b). Children of transsexual parents. In: D. Di Ceglie & D. Freedman (Eds.), *A Stranger In My Own Body. Atypical Gender Identity Development and Mental Health*. London: Karnac.

Di Ceglie, D. (2000). Gender identity disorder in young people. *Advances in Psychiatric Treatment, 6*: 458–466.

Royal College of Psychiatrists (1998). *Gender Identity Disorders in Children and Adolescents—Guidance For Management*, Council Report CR63. London: Royal College of Psychiatrists.

Stoller, R. J. (1968). *Sex and Gender*, Vol. 1. New York: Science House.

# CHAPTER FIVE

# Transference and countertransference in group analysis with gender dysphoric patients

*Estela V. Welldon*

The term "Transsexualism" was first used by the endocrinologist and sexologist Harry Benjamin in 1953 to describe a condition in which both men and women have fantasies and beliefs of belonging to the other gender which become more and more overwhelming and intrusive with an almost quasi-delusional quality of this belief.

This "quasi-delusional" quality has been eloquently described by Hakeem (2007).

The *ICD-10* diagnostic guidelines for F64.0 define Transsexualism as:

> A desire to live and be accepted as a member of the opposite sex, usually accompanied by a sense of discomfort with, or inappropriateness of, one's anatomic sex and a wish to have hormonal treatment and surgery to make one's body as congruent as possible with the preferred sex.

It goes on to detail the diagnostic guidelines as:

> For this diagnosis to be made, the transsexual identity should have been present persistently for at least 2 years, and must not be a

symptom of another mental disorder, such as schizophrenia, or associated with any intersexed, genetic, or sex chromosomal abnormality.

In the past, practitioners in the field associated this condition with latent homosexuality and different sorts of transvestism. The definition of transsexualism has developed with the increasing trend of the population to seek specific help for this condition. Transsexuals feel they are a woman trapped in a man's body, and vice versa.

As such, transsexualism is a complicated and complex situation, which, in lay terms, is a self-made diagnosis with a "self-prescribed" treatment.

There are differential diagnoses to make in the three cross-dressing disorders. Briefly, in transvestism it is used compulsively, as a perversion, for purposes of sexual arousal; in practitioners of drag, the cross-dressing is professionally used for entertaining purposes; and transsexualist individuals do it because of an intense wish to belong to the opposite sex and a need to reassure themselves that they do.

The patient's conviction that they require surgical reassignment to the correct sex/gender is unshakeable, with little evidence other than their certainty. In this sense, it resembles delusional thinking requiring a radical action. This is usually made in a stern, certain, and immovable way, which, when faced with professionals, produces in the latter most times a negative reaction, born of insecurity and confusion regarding these patients' :irrational: demands of having a "sex reassignment". In other words, males experience an urgent need to become "women", and women to become "men".

Chiland (2005, p. 15) accurately says, "To this mad request, physicians have responded with a mad offer". The person affected by this condition experiences a sense of alienation or dislocation between mind and body which lacks a specific psychopathology. They do not experience a psychological conflict within themselves and rarely consult a professional; when they do, it is for the exclusive purpose of demanding a sex reassignment operation.

These gender dysphoria patients at times believe themselves to be transsexuals, although they experience a strong ambivalence regarding their gender such that this internal conflict is massively projected to the outside world. For example, at times the person experiences his or her first urge to consult a practitioner who might facilitate the actual "sex change".

When this "self-prescribed treatment" gets a second positive opinion from the medical profession, the person might experience panic and fly in the opposite direction to consult another practitioner, whom he or she believes will be against the proposed operation, such as a psychotherapist or psychoanalyst. This is his way of projecting the opposing sides of his inner conflict on to the outside, obtaining two different sets of clinics, doctors, or other professionals with contrasting views.

This was observed by Limentani (1979) when he remarks that, from the early 1970s, the Portman Clinic had countless numbers of referrals of transsexual patients, creating a most peculiar position of operating a sort of two-way traffic with the Charing Cross Gender Clinic regarding these patients own polarizing offers and demands. The latter, at the time, liberally and casually provided, under the guidance of a most eager senior consultant, radical treatment to those who felt the desire or need to "change sex", as it was then called. Some undecided "transsexual" patients used to react with much fear and anxiety at the offer of an operation as a quick panacea to their awful body and psychic pain. In this case, they would retreat with equal rapidity to consult the Portman Clinic, offering the safety of exclusive "talk therapy". At other times, the opposite process was in operation: following consultations with the Portman, patients left feeling angry and frustrated by their perceived lack of sensitivity and denial of the staff to collude with any radical treatment, and indignant about not only the long-term commitment, but also demands involved in any offer of psychotherapy, and off they went to Charing Cross Clinic. Quite often, this pattern clearly revealed their profound ambivalence. Some of them gained a degree of insight about their mixed feelings, and a therapeutic intervention had been unwittingly created.

In this chapter, I provide illustrative clinical material to describe this condition. First, I use narratives from a therapeutic group, which was particularly different from the other already established groups at the Portman Clinic. Those changes, which will be described later on, encompassed not only differences in the composition of the group, but also in the way it was conducted, for both patients and staff. This group created a precedent in that the group had co-therapists, a male and female, since all other groups were functioning with a single therapist. The reasons for this are outlined under "Aim 2" in this paper, and more extensively in Welldon (1996) in Cordess and Cox.

I hope that these examples will convey the burdens in the accomplishment of understanding important transference issues of the psychodynamics of the internal world of the transsexual patient.

Person (1994) supports Stoller's ideas, which suggested that gender identity precedes gender role and sexual orientation in development and that it organizes them, not the reverse. Hence, it is vital to keep in mind Stoller's (1968) terminology, in that "sex" is biology and "gender" is social.

Second, I describe the process of massification (Hopper, 2003) as a defence against the aggregation phenomenon based on annihilation anxieties derived from body dysfunctions, such as self harm, and eating disorders, which most patients presented. Actually and ironically, in the eventual introduction in the group of a woman who wanted to have a "sex change" to become a man, she was perceived by the male-to-female (known as mtf) group members as a man in gender terms. She, by wanting to have a penis, made the mtf members react to her as a gender intrusion and not as a sexual person. Even unconsciously, transsexual patients know the difference between gender and sex! It is interesting to note that Juliet Mitchell (2006a,b) has come to believe that the concept of gender, first introduced by Stoller in the mid 1960s, may be the most important conceptual contribution to the subject to date.

Third, I describe my own dream and my co-therapists dream of this conundrum. This illustrates how affected we clinicians are in our countertransferential processes.

Limentani (1979) regards

the transsexual syndrome as a personality and characterological disaster which cannot be corrected by mutilating operations which are often carried out in response to suicide threats amounting to blackmail. Unlike many other psychiatric conditions where the patient is clearly attempting to achieve a cure, here the patient requires the cure to be achieved by involving others, who are asked to play into the fantasy of adding to a pretension a distorted body, often a caricature of the real thing.

This condition, according to Anna Motz (personal communication) may be likened to Munchausen's, enlisting the medical professionals to inflict harm and thereby enacting perversion against the medical body, as well as one's own.

It is relevant here to mention the revolutionary and apt suggestion made by Argentieri (2006), who notices that psychoanalysts are often concerned with and use sophisticated concepts in the understanding of these patients, who are sadly already psychologically damaged. She argues that an efficient way to pre-empt collusive attitudes from the medical profession would be to provide them, the surgical medical teams, instead of the patients, with therapy groups where psychodynamic insight and understanding would be applied prior to any surgical proceedings.

Chiland (2005) maintains a sympathetic, although courageous and non-collusive approach to these patients in their quest for the "sex exchange", facing them with the unreality of this request. She declares, with eloquence, "Yet a therapist cannot but be the ambassador of reality: maintaining the illusion would mean going from illusion to delusion".

Often, these patients have suffered in their early childhood from faulty, perverting mothering, in which they have been made, not only to be dressed as, but to feel as if they actually belong to, the opposite gender. Their mothers have often been cruel and sadistic in pursuing their own wishes for this "chosen" baby. At other times, this baby has been a replacement baby, after the early death of a sibling.

Lothstein (1979) stresses the role of the mother in the etiology of transsexualism in his studies of the mothers of male and female transsexuals. According to him,

> These mothers are unable to tolerate their sons' separation and individuation via masculine identifications and remain attached to their sons via feminine identifications. They seem to perceive the male child's gender separateness as a threat to their own personal integrity. [p. 122]

Lothstein describes a process that operates in the upbringing of daughters who become transsexuals:

These mothers also experience their daughters' prolonged and continued identifications as a threat to their personal integrity. By actively pushing their daughters away from feminine identifications, they seem to be protecting themselves from symbiotic fusion and regression. Our clinical data suggest that their daughters' male identifications may be partially defensive, to ward off both their and their mothers' murderous wishes toward each other. [p. 221]

He then hypothesizes that the mother's

proneness to disrupt one of her child's gender-identities will vary as a function of the sex of the child, the stresses in her marriage, her current relationship to her own mother, and the current status of her *bisexual* conflict. [p. 222, my italics]

I remarked (Welldon, 1988, p. 68) "These children comply with their mothers' wishes as their only way of survival and in so doing they create a false sense of self with structural ego defects and ego weaknesses".

Greer (1999) argues that

There is a witness to the transsexual scrip, a witness who is never consulted. She is the person who built the transsexual body of her own flesh and brought it up as her son or daughter, the transsexual worst enemy, his/her mother. When a man decides to spend his life impersonating his mother (like Norman Bates in *Psycho*) it is as if he murders her and gets away with it, proving at a stroke that there was nothing to her. [p. 74]

None the less, she alludes to the aggression of the transsexual in his attempt to embody her, and there may be some truth in this, although it is only part of the story.

Greer is not the only author who links transsexualism with Norman Bates in *Psycho* and its importance in the mother–transsexual boy. Thurer (2005) cites the importance of the fantasy of fusion in dealing with problems of separation–individuation from the mother and acutely remarks,

Like Norman Bates, incorporating some aspect of her into himself, or in the most extreme instance, by reversing his gender identity from male to female. In this way the mother and child become "one" and the danger of separation is nullified. Note that the child does not suffer from castration anxiety; on the contrary, he suffers from anxiety unless he is castrated. [p. 183]

These mothers have been themselves victims of faulty mothering. This is why the study of the family constellation is basic to the understanding of this complex problem. Sometimes patients feel consciously or unconsciously both protective and vindictive towards their mothers. In Winnicott's understanding of severe psychopathology, "It is the environment which causes the recipient of its impact to muster various defences". Mitchell further adds that, in cases of gender dysphoria, the boy's belief that he is a girl corresponds to his own mother's expectation of his or her gender. In other words, in transferential terms, the "environment mother", has becomes the "mad mother". That is one of the important issues that make interpretation of the transference impossible to achieve.

We thought that group analytical therapy might be the choice treatment considering the difficulties encountered in individual sessions and the following were our treatment objectives.

To allow a process of identification with others rather than isolation.
To achieve a degree of self acceptance rather than judgement and persecution.
To achieve a better sense of social reality through the working situation of the group.

### The impact of this in the presentation–engagement of patients in psychotherapy

In my experience, these patients are likely to attend a few sessions and stop coming after a short while. This is followed later on with requests for further sessions, even years later. They usually express an interest to see women diagnosticians. This is unconsciously motivated by either revenge against mother or an attempt to seek her approval–participation, corresponding to their own mother's expectation of their gender.

It could also be seen as an avoidance of seeing a man because of a phantasied attack from a male therapist in their search to get rid of their male genitalia, a desired/wanted castration. At times, the search for a sex change operation in men in their late forties is the expression of a middle-age crisis in which a more attractive and youthful image is pursued, and at other times unconscious psychotic mechanisms are at stake. All requests for body "mutilations" may be the tip of the iceberg for very disturbing conditions in which a severe self-destructive aim is at the core.

The account I give in this paper is of the first year of life of this group, from its original conception. This was run by me and a male co therapist, a graduate from the Institute of Group Analysis. All names of patients are fictitious in order to preserve confidentiality.

(This group, as from my retirement in 2001, was taken and is still run by a former trainee of mine, Dr Az Hakeem, who has written about his experiences running this group. As a result of the success of this group in terms of benefits felt by patients and referrals of such patients to the group, Dr Hakeem is shortly setting up a second specialist gender dysphoria group within the clinic.)

To start with, the group was composed of only men who felt they were born in the wrong gender but were undecided about taking the route of gender reassignment. Later on they were joined by women who suffered from similar predicaments. The group therapists, a woman and a man, began the enterprise in a spirit of research, and psychodynamic exploration. We did not expect much and always kept in mind Stoller's assertion: "The general rule that applies to the treatment of the transsexual is that no matter what one does—including nothing—it will be wrong" (1968, p. 247).

In fact, at the end of that year, towards the end of the 1990s, we were left somewhat emotionally wounded, professionally humbled, with more questions than answers regarding everything including our own gender identities, but we were ultimately also strengthened by this experience.

The curious system, already described, of "two-way traffic" referrals to both our Clinic and Charing Cross Gender Clinic of gender dysphoria patients made us aware of the intense inner dilemmas encountered by these patients. Keeping this in mind, we decided to offer them an extended, prolonged, exploratory diagnostic assessment, as suggested by Dr Limentani much earlier on in my career, when he became my supervisor on my joining the Portman staff.

I thought that this could be achieved by means of group therapy meetings, especially since a new staff member, trained at the Institute of Group Analysis, had joined the Clinic.

We had to act quickly, with tact and caution, keeping in mind that the Clinic was never too happy to offer group therapy. Also, there was some consensus within the Clinic that we should no longer be offering treatment to such patients, on the basis that, since they were not considered as suffering from perversions, they were not within the remit of our work.

Hence, in this the approach we adopted, there were some clear differences from our then usual practice:

- patient population—requiring a different approach/strategy;
- co-therapists as opposed to single therapist;
- co-therapists of different training and approach.

We decided to offer them weekly group psychotherapy with the following characteristics and aims.

1. To offer gender dysphoric patients a forum and a space to discuss freely their own feelings about their dilemmas regarding mind–body splits without being, or without experiencing being, pushed into either male or female "solutions". In doing so, we had the expectation of learning more about these conditions from a dynamic viewpoint, to ascertain more specifically the differences between sexual perversions and gender dysphoric conditions, which would provide us with material for publications and research. In the words of Chiland (2005, p. 22) "I want to explore with the patient who or what he or she is and leave as many doors open as possible".

2. This new challenge needed innovative thinking and as such it seemed "obviously" a good idea to offer co-therapists of different genders for people who are so deeply confused about their own gender identities. This created a precedent, since it had been our policy that all therapy groups were to be run by single therapists because of the potential risk involving violence due to the psychopathology of our patient population. Most, if not all, come from broken homes and have been subjected to much neglect and abuse. In our view, they could

easily feel provoked and humiliated when confronted with a couple of therapists. The few attempts to run groups with co-therapists have consistently ended in disaster. In these few instances, the consistent outcome has been the regrettable break up of the co-therapists' working relationship. This represents the repetition, in transferential terms, of the skills these patients have at making the therapists re-enact their own histories of fighting and neglectful parents.

This strongly contrasts with the countertransferential response obtained with our particular group, in which a closeness of the co-therapists was the result. This apparent closeness was in contrast with our differing backgrounds, which is outlined below. The further exploration and research of these clinical findings would be very important in the elucidation of these patients' early psycho aetiology with the corresponding object-relationship with their carers and the possible differentiation between perversions and gender dysphoric states already proposed by Stoller.

3.    Our enthusiasm for our project made us overlook the important differences of our personal and professional backgrounds, which, in more than one way, could seem to be replicating the stereotyped Stoller family dynamics of the transsexual patient. For example, the male therapist was younger, more inexperienced, and junior to the female therapist. His own training was less confrontational , making him appear "soft" and "sweet" while the woman was ready to offer interpretations of the negative transference, due to her Kleinian training. We became aware that this style of transferential interpretations did make very little sense to this patient population. It is relevant in this context to consider Chiland's observation (2004, p. 16) "Transsexuals stage everything in the theatre of the body and nothing in that of the psyche".

In no time my male colleague, who had felt "excited and privileged" at the prospect of sharing a group with me, became rather irritated and frustrated. Our own different techniques were, at the beginning, far more evident, and at times produced some degree of tension, but soon after we began to notice changes in our own styles which led to a better integration of our working together. So, from a potential for fragmentation, we were able to achieve a good degree of cohesion.

There were unexpected ways the patients felt provoked by the so-called "normality" in our stereotyped cultural gender assignations. For example, the two-way "traffic" was also re-enacted in our Clinic, where there are two doors, one marked Men and the other Women, which confront all who enter the front hall of the Portman Clinic. In this way, the Clinic conforms to a fundamental ordering of human nature that is ordinarily and continuously conveyed by social structures.

The people who came to this group, however, felt unable to fit into either one of these categories. Those who had used the male toilets bitterly complained of the absence of a mirror. Was this just narcissism, or an expression of the lack of inner reflection to what they felt they looked like? Talking about their difficulties (which are sometimes experienced as exciting) in using the public toilet of their choice, it was revealed that several have found a solution by using those toilets which are reserved for the disabled. Far from feeling consciously disabled, however, our group seemed to have released a sense of indignation at having been so unfairly treated by fate, by society, by life. They complained bitterly also against the therapists, who not only represent established social values, but, on a more personal level, by their apparent gender contentment, were experienced as the fundamental oppressors of those burdened by their gender discontent. There is male and female, biologically, and we began to learn how much we have assumed that personality is constructed in a similar dichotomy. Remembering Winnicott's formulation that, in all of us, as from birth there are male and female elements, we may have to revisit our long-held belief that there is absence of symbolic thinking in transsexualism. It may be we who are factually acting in a concrete way! Our group has taught us that there are innumerable gender identities. Greer (1999, p. 65) acutely asserts that "Sex change surgery is profoundly conservative in that it reinforces sharply contrasting gender roles by shaping individuals to fit them".

Argentieri (2006) stresses that the transsexual thinking process, even if limited to the core gender identity, it is linked to the concretization of the body and it is unconcerned with the playing of fantasies.

The obstinacy in finding a solution only at the biological level is a symptom of their inability to have access to the symbolic processes and it has roots in a pre-symbolic stage of incomplete separation between self and not self. [my translation]

From the very start of the sessions, all and each held the determination that only a physical transformation of the body and to "become a woman" would suffice to provide some repair to their emotional damage. Sessions proceeded with each speaking as if from a narcissistic island. On the other hand, there was much in common between the members of the group: hostility to parents, to society and its strictures, the long-standing sense of being a misfit, and frequent reference to self-damage. Therefore, bridges were built.

Throughout the first year, tremendous hostility was aroused if the therapists made comments at all to do with family, relationships, and especially, mother. Dismissed as predictable clichés, "A-Level Freudian claptrap", these were also felt as intolerable attacks on the basic position of group members. Horror was expressed at the masculine body. Being "female" was seen as the only way to be at peace; anything else was experienced as traumatic. This was a homogeneous group with a language of its own. We were introduced to code words, such as "transitioning" (to the other sex), "being read", (if cross-dressed in public), RLT (real life training as the opposite sex), TS, TV, MTF, FTM, and so on. They talked of changes from "transgender" to "transsexual", to "intersex", to "inbetweenie", "gender outlaw". Somebody talked about their "feeling like being in the waiting room", meaning that they were not sure exactly where they were coming from or where they were going to. Sentences such as "what's the woman I would like to be?", or "I was in love with the body that I didn't have", all seemingly indicated a sort of intersex situation which did not correspond either to the male not to the female. This secret society of our group members seemed to compensate for the otherwise lonely preoccupations, but isolation persisted and intimate relationships (sexual or otherwise) seemed impossible. For the therapists to observe and comment on this was experienced as rubbing salt into the wound. This clinical feature has been extensively studied by Chiland and others.

Since transferential interpretations were out of question, and the body characteristics are of such paramount importance, I had an inspired idea of making tentative interpretations to do with the damage inflicted to their bodies: sometimes wounds were raw and open, left without any care. Weight, eating disorders, and self-harm also took my attention, and I began to make remarks concerning their bodies which were taken seriously, but these were just like drops in the ocean. I found extremely useful Mitchell's (2006a,b) discussion of Winnicott's work in understanding gender/social sex and its interaction with the environment mother. She specifically writes,

> The person who maims their own body through such acts as cutting or disordered eating would be attacking the environment-as-(not-good-enough) body. Maiming is thus as a-social as stealing—both are protests against traumatizing environments in their subject's past history.

In Anna Motz's words, "Self-harm is a defence against intimacy, binding a woman to her own body to the exclusion of others" (Motz, 2008, p. 230).

My co therapist was soon disappointed by the acute lack of creativity in the group. Their preoccupations with concrete facts such as hormone treatment, surgery, and electrolysis for hair removal reflected an absurd, fixed idea of "becoming a woman". Their lack of symbolism induced feelings of disillusionment and hopelessness in both of us. My co-therapist's golden dream of working with me, the senior and very experienced clinician, quickly began to fade away and he saw me as ineffective and useless. It was as though our union had created an insatiable monster of a baby, for whom nothing was right and so destroyed any further intercourse between us. Thus, the experience began to feel like an attack on both our own gender identity as revealed by our respective dreams, which will be described later on.

We had two early drop-outs, who managed to convey that the group was worthless.

Differences between the therapists were highlighted, and my co-therapist felt the stress of being so denigrated. He found my technique rather strict, as I declined to answer questions or give explanations to the group. His inclination was to offer more ego support and to interpret unconscious content less in the early stages, and at times he responded in a more open manner to the group. But soon he corrected this, since he felt he did not want to be seen as the "nice" or the "soft" one. But it was hard for him to escape the role of being less important because of my senior position in the Clinic and also having been responsible for conducting some of the assessments. In preparing some members for the group, I made it clear that they were not to attend sessions in women's clothes. The rule became a source of bitter complaints throughout. My co-therapist felt in danger that he might present a compromised model of masculinity in becoming a weak and uncertain kind of father, unable to compensate for the unfulfilled masculinity of mother, just as described by Stoller in the transsexual family dynamic. Meantime, in becoming aware of his conflicts, I waited for his interventions, and took care to make comments that reinforced, or positively developed, his own. In retrospect, we both wonder if it may have been this very closeness between the two of us that was so unbearable to members of the group. As the sessions became repetitive and seemingly unconstructive, drowsiness became a continuing problem for the therapists.

My co-therapist was by now resentful of my presence and began to withdraw, feeling uncomfortable about his resentment towards me, and felt "presumptuously" that if it had been his group, there would not have been such difficulties. So he experienced an acute sense of shame when I told him of my dream in which he seemed to be joining in the group's sexualized attack on me.

When I was absent he felt confronted by his lack of knowledge of some of the Clinic's routine and procedures. When I returned, the group displayed outright hostility, attacking my appearance, my manner, and my silence; "She should be kicked out," said a patient. The hostility to my co-therapist was more subtly expressed, with flirtatious remarks about his appearance, though when he said anything he sustained outright derision and mockery. In an obvious way, they were experiencing me as the unwanted, intrusive female who has everything and is blissfully unaware of her "good luck". But, looking at deeper layers, their flirtatious approach to my male therapist conveyed their seeing him as a woman, an inferior one, almost a part of me. Their different approach to us could also be seen as trying to create a fighting, and eventually destroyed, impotent couple. He felt most embarrassed by the insults to myself and did not know how to respond. He spoke about the envy of us both, but his comments were rejected. For example,

"It is like a glass wall separates you both from the rest of us. Occasionally you came out from behind it and say something."

"You don't really have anything to do with the group. You are together."

"It is as though there is electricity between you."

"You are irrelevant to the group."

"Your comments are completely unhelpful, and meaningless."

"You seem so happy, so smug, in your gender, why should you have anything to say about us?"

We tried to think about the "meaninglessness" of our contributions. Our communications to the group were based on an assumption that the gender dysphoria was a condition, something that needed to be understood and solved, a problem. In the group's view it was a given, and unchangeable. The more specifically we tried to address feelings about gender, the more our comments would be rejected. On one occasion, for example, after complaints about women having things that they feel they cannot have, my co-therapist suggested that there were also feelings about the woman's body, and in particular the vagina. He never was given the chance to articulate and finish his thoughts, being interrupted by hoots of derision, which I interpreted as a reaction to tremendous anxiety, but his comments were dismissed by the group as "off the wall" remarks that had little or *nothing* to do with the group's discussions.

The less the therapists intervened, the more it seemed that questioning and thinking was possible. However, my co-therapist felt this to be a very unstable base for any group; according to him, the presence of the therapists should represent the purpose and setting of the group. If we were the sole objects of hate and had to be made completely redundant, then the group would have to end. Instead, I felt that we were the containers for their anger, even rage, at what they considered to be the most terrible injustice inflicted on them from birth, so, although painful to us, it was therapeutic for our patients. But my "understanding" and tolerance soon were replaced by anger and despondency at discovering that they were spending long periods of time talking after the group sessions on the outside stairs. This acting out seemed to emanate from a feeling of sameness and an inability to separate on the face of similar predicaments. This was quite different from the other groups, in which people do not feel at all like hanging around together. As we can see, a process of massification (Hopper, 2003, p. 94).

Further denigration came to the fore when one member offered the others an "alternative" to the therapy sessions by inviting them to reconvene at his home, where they could wear women's clothes, relax, and have a drink. This was a serious attempt to break down the therapeutic boundaries established in their initial therapeutic contract with the Clinic. By then we had resigned ourselves to giving transferential interpretations, but this invitation was revealing of their terror of acknowledging relationships, particularly related to transference to therapists rather than to one another, hence the need to have own "groups" without boundaries, or real parental couple.

Towards the end of the year two dropped out, one ostensibly because of travel difficulties, and did not even bother to respond to offers of help from the clinic. The other because, he said, he had decided that he would go for "the operation" and felt that he was completely misunderstood by the therapists. In a letter, he complained of a lack of direction and leadership by the therapists, ignoring the fact that all our comments were dismissed. Sessions became desultory and repetitive; the therapists were oppressed by drowsiness. The last meeting of the year was attended by no one except ourselves, left, so it felt, to commiserate with only each other. In a way, we could say that through this gender-shaping mutilating process we had been left without any kind of charge, energy, or excitement, as though all libidinal energy had been drained. The attempt to destroy the parental couple and render it impotent had finally been achieved.

A great heaviness and gloom confronted and embraced both of us at the end of 1998. "Now is the winter of our discontent" represented our deep frustration and despair at our experience of working together as co-therapists of a gender dysphoric group, composed exclusively of m-to-f group members.

Whereas my co-therapist felt as if he was failing the group, I felt instead angry with the patients, and almost ready for the first time to give up the group.

Although I was familiar with the enormous complications and risky situations encountered in applying group analysis to social and sexual deviancies, I had never felt like giving up a group before.

Two new members joined, and in January 1999 our mood and expectations changed considerably with the introduction of the first female-to-male (ftm) member. Hilary was a rather heavily built, butch-looking young woman of twenty-three, an artist who has been in a relationship for many years with a lesbian woman. Her main aim in joining was to explore her feelings in getting to know whether she was a "true" transsexual. When she first came to the group she let the others know that she had already been to other groups, which she found to be rather irrelevant and a waste of time because their focus had been either hormone treatment or surgery. Former members, all mtf, were rather ambivalent towards her as a group. For example, one member of around her age was rather pleased about her being there, but he himself, and the other group members, were dismissive about her and spent most of the time trying to figure out what to do about a letter from an absent member. The real irony here is that Hilary was experienced as a gender and not as a sex. She was felt as an intrusive, shafted penis, able to create primary scene anxieties.

There were moments of more constructive work. The new members did not relish the attacks on the therapists. It was like an illumination when one group member said, "Why are we so angry and so bitter to them?" Another said, "After all, we have to find our own answers. Actually, this suits me better. I don't want to be given answers. I would automatically distrust them." A bond between group members as fellow sufferers was developing as they said things to each other that could be said to no one else outside the group:

"I want to see myself as a naked woman . . ."

Each had had breakdowns of one sort or another, and the feelings of despair and hopelessness were shared. The trauma of being the "wrong sex" was mitigated, so it seemed, by the act of sharing. Emotional attunement was beginning, as well as a deeper questioning of themselves;

"Yes, but what kind of woman do you want to be?"

"The question is not so much how can I be female, but how can I be male."

"What kind of sexual relationship could I have if I 'transition'?"

These were revelations that denoted an attempt to give up some of the rigid and safe concrete thinking for an exploration to some symbolic wonderment. They wanted to explore in more detail all different possibilities, but sadly, this did not stay for too long, as is shown in the next example.

In our therapy groups we have a long tradition of writing letters to absent members. This represents the stage when the group has taken possession of its own power and it is marked by their readiness to compose a letter during a session as a group task. In other words, at the inception of any therapeutic group, authority and power are with the therapists. But as soon as members feel a sense of belonging to the group, a positive division of labour takes place. Authority remains with the therapists (they are the ones who determine the holidays, the length of the group treatment, etc.). Group members instead become aware that the continuity of the group is their own responsibility and as such it becomes *their* group. Writing letters to absent members, during the group session, demonstrates how they can work together, achieving independence, coherence, and cohesiveness, factors determining their own sense of power.

With this particular group it was a very difficult task to accomplish. For example, one of the members took it on as an individual to answer an absent member by writing a letter from his own home and brought it in at a group session, which happened to be the first Hilary attended. The letter was typed and ready for people to sign.

When interpretations were made to the effect that he had taken something away from the group, he became angry and upset about the lack of appreciation on the part of the therapists in not recognizing his own work and initiative. All these litigations continued in the following session. Hilary, despite her apparent aplomb, was disappointed in her expectations from the group. I believe that she was also rather put out by the fact that she was witness to a frontal attack from the group members towards the therapists in a consistently sneering way. She was not that willing or enthusiastic about joining the angry attack of the other members on the two therapists, who were seen as" straight people", unable to understand them and who had no idea about the difficulties or the problems they were facing. She represented a disappointment in female idealization and the group responded with an envious attack on her, like I had experienced throughout the whole year from the m-to-f members. However, she was able to deal with this and confront them with their lack of insight.

A few weeks later she did not come, and instead sent a letter saying that she did not intend to come back to the group because "it was not the right time for her to be there". Everyone appeared to be hit by an important sense of loss; such had been her own input to the group with many insightful comments. The therapists shared the same sense of loss. I, myself, felt devastated, since I had great emotional investment in her entry to the group. She had brought a different climate in which discussion of feelings had become the norm; she often confronted herself and others in her quest for her own truth. After discussion, they decided to answer her all together, as a whole. This was followed by the successful outcome of getting Hilary to come back. This gave the group a turning point in its development. Not only had they succeeded in writing a letter, but also, in doing so, they had unwittingly admitted almost inadvertently, for the first time, their favourable response to the group dynamics in saying how important the group experience was for them. This was a kind of healthy symbol of transformation of loss; they were able to retrieve someone or something that has been damaged and restore her to life, some sort of a parallel to the fantasy of transformation from loss to belonging: they wrote in positive terms of how much they had been able to obtain from the sessions. This surprised us, since we were not prepared for such a positive statement, never made before.

It was fortunate that when Hilary came back, the second female-to-male (ftm), Debbie, had already joined the group. An immediate change of situation took place, in which Hilary felt much more at ease, although at times Hilary was prone to use Debbie to provide her with much information, getting some excitement from the fact that Debbie seemed to be more and more adamant in her pursuing of a "change". Hilary, instead, decided that she was actually not a transsexual, but perhaps transgender or, more possibly so, a butch, lesbian person. At times she also reflected on the possibility of her leaving the group since it was exclusively composed of trans-sexuals, but we were against this since the main goal was to discuss all problems in relation to gender dysphoria. A third ftm was later admitted to the group, and with her inclusion the attendance became more regular.

After the arrival of the ftms, our feelings towards the group changed.

As I mentioned earlier this group produced a degree of close-ness and mutual trust in that they were able to disclose under-standing and our reactions to whatever was happening in the group and to specific patients in the group. This was rather gratify-ing, since we, as therapists, could talk and explore our own feelings in relation to our working together and to our genders.

One of the most frequent themes that they were able to tackle more openly was about the members' and some of their own relatives' eating disorders. For example, Hilary continued being periodically bulimic whereas Debbie and Peter were anorectic, Sebastian's mother also had a history of anorexia. There could be a symbolic linking to their confusion of genders, since anorexia is a condition frequently associated with women, with concomitant aggression to the self and also as an attack against the mother. According to Anna Motz (2008, p. 266): "anorexia nervosa . . . reflects unconscious murderous feelings both towards the mother and towards the self". There was also a reference to their inability and difficulties in taking any nurturance offered by both therapists, because of their enormous suspicion and envy towards the mater-nal nurturing body. It was gratifying that, from eating disorders, they began tentatively to talk about depression. For the first time they were acknowledging feelings of depression; even Sebastian, who appealed to massive manic defences, manifested in much contempt and denigration towards the therapists, began for the first time to acknowledge feeling depressed and having suicidal ideation. That was a fundamental shift in their dynamics in that an acknowledgement of what was really missing was evident.

Mitchell's ideas and concepts are particularly illuminating in understanding this attempt to reach a depressive position. I found Mitchell's project of using, combining, and encompassing the works and conceptualizations used by Winnicott of the "environment mother", together with those of Klein on the depressive position, and Bowlby on deprivation in the understanding of gender, as a way to obtain a psychoanalytical view which would be wider and different from just sex (biology) plus gender (the social). The individual who has been deprived, with an impoverished early environment (environment mother), attacks/steals in order to have the environment withstand this, demonstrating some hope that the environment has something to provide. There is a connection between stealing in Winnicott's paper "The antisocial tendency" (1956), in making the environment crucial with its present response or hoped-for response as the outcome of deprivation (Bowlby), and absence of mourning (Klein), with concomitant inability to reach the depressive position.

The presence of women in the patient group meant that we, as a heterosexual co-therapist couple, could be mirrored, maybe reducing the envy of the two of us as the only "real" couple.

The group contained at this point both elements of heterogeneity and homogeneity: the former, in the sense of being composed of the two genders, brought about a process of socialization and a climate of openness in talking about their feelings. The homogeneity, represented by the fact that they were all gender dysphoric, produced a consistent acting-out trait.

Chiland (2005, p. 17) remarks,

> The loathing of the genital organs—the penis in biological males—must be emphasized. Biological females have a comparable loathing of the breast. At clinical level, it is impossible to say what it is in a transsexual that comes first in time, importance, and existential causality—the loathing of his own sex or the desire to belong to the opposite sex.

Of course, the intriguing trait was the combination of two different groups of people, each of whom having what the other wanted to get rid of, producing rich, bizarre, and, at times, rather awkward situations. There was a constant awareness about what they wanted to get rid of, especially the men; they wanted to be rid of all that they had, and in a way, the vagina did not appear to be such a promising feature to acquire. Now this was interesting, because the women wanted to get rid of their breasts and found them to be a rather awful thing to have, and experienced great depression when the menses appeared. These feelings of revulsion were just as strong as the mtf experienced towards their penises. It is interesting that the culturally usual psychological characteristics of each gender remained, described as follows.

The introduction of the ftm members brought a sort of stereotyped version of the two genders: in other words, even though these people experienced very serious problems in relation to their gender identity, the men were still very much talking about the outside world, externalizing their own conflicts in the outside world with an enormous amount of projective identification, whereas the women were much more ready to talk about their own feelings, to admit different conflictual views about themselves. They were far more ready to talk about themselves and their relationship to others, including their family members.

The letter writing seemed to produce in the group members a feeling of having a great sense of power in their achievement of having Hilary back in the group. This, and their admission of having been helped by attending sessions, created a turning point in which they felt much more in charge of their own destinies. Their complaining about the lack of guidance and lack of understanding from the therapists began to fade away and not to be as vigorous as before. The vicious attacks on me as a woman diminished, and the flirtation with, and teasing of, the male therapist were also reduced in frequency.

At the end of the first year, my co-therapist found himself asking what it meant to be male. He wondered: "Is it only to be understood in terms of an opposition to female? That certainly makes an answer easier to find, but is this a kind of truth that is anything more than a constructed social reality? Was there something that our patients could find, a female in themselves, that could fulfil the constant yearning that was experienced?" He dreamed that he was angry with the group, and walked out, only to be called back and criticized by me. "She was laughing at me with a group of women. She walked away from me, and, try as I might, I could not catch up with her." In our discussions, we wondered if our dreams did represent a glimpse for us of the profound incompleteness experienced by our patients, who could never find in the other what they lacked in themselves.

During that year, I, as a female therapist, felt most times that I was used as the target for much envy and hostility. This is a common feature in our work, which I am used to and welcome, since I believe that the expression of those negative feelings is part of a healthy process of incipient maturation and development of trust. This situation, though, was quite different from any other. I felt got at to the extent of consistently feeling sleepy and drowsy, a feeling shared by my co-therapist. A joke that we discussed was how our patients had succeeded in sending both of us to sleep together. In this case they were re-enacting a primary scene from which they were left out and alone, without the "intrusion" of the parental figures. I felt ferociously attacked by the members, without any of the redeeming traits which often appear in the other groups. A few times I had fantasies of my co-therapist joining in, being myself all on my own, the target of enormous sadism, as if a fox hunted by a pack. This materialized in a dream I had when I was absent from the group and it was conducted by my co-therapist.

> I arrive late to the room where the session is taking place. The room is in a state of disorder with the group members moving around disruptively. Then, to my horror, I see that my co-therapist has joined them, and I feel there is a concerted attack on me. I also noticed that my spectacles case is trodden on and broken. This was made out of tortoiseshell (I must reveal that the Spanish word for conch is used in a most vulgar and pejorative way, and its literal translation is "cunt").

In these dreams there is a painful realization of how threatened we had both felt, regardless of our apparent "closeness" and sense of solidarity. We both felt denigrated and being made subjects of humiliation. In my own dream, my broken glasses indicate I am unable to see what is going on, hence, unable to offer any help. The next impending disaster is for my conch to be smashed up!

There is an antagonistic symmetry with my co-therapist's dream of me being angry when I succeeded in getting him back after his walking out of the group, only to be criticized and laughed at by me, together with a group of angry women, and his being unable to catch up with me. Not only did this leave him wondering what means to be male, but he also added, "Is it only to be understood in terms of an opposition to female? That certainly makes an answer easier to find, but is this a kind of truth that is anything more than a constructed social reality? Was there something that our patients could find, a female in themselves, that could fulfil the constant yearning that was experienced?"

This left us with what might have been a glimpse for us of the profound incompleteness experienced by our patients, who could never find in the other what they lacked in themselves.

By now we felt more aware of the complexities encountered by our patients, responsible for their apparent lack of symbolic thought replaced by concrete thinking, denial, and aggression, which accounted for their intense envious attacks on our gender identities. We became more confident and alert. Our sleepiness had certainly disappeared with a renewed sense of potency.

I am reminded here of Person's thinking (2005, p. 1056):

> we cannot privilege biology if we take into account transgender choices, for example those of transsexuals, who cannot tolerate their sexual organs despite the absence of any evidence of hormonal imbalance, and who seek surgery so as to approach as closely as possible the appearance of the sex they desire to be. . . . We still do not know with any degree of certainty the varying degrees of biological, developmental, and cultural contributions to sexual object choice or gender of self-identification.

## Conclusions

I believe were able to meet the limited aims proposed at the start of this experience, such as patients being able to identify with others and share their own predicaments with openness. After processing their tremendous fears of persecution and inability to look into themselves, they began to question their choices and to discern what would be best for each of them, albeit in a tentative way.

Initially, the therapists' countertransference replicated the patients' intense fears of being misunderstood, judged, and persecuted in an intensive concrete way by feeling useless, powerless, and, at times, sharing a degree of confusion about their own roles. The group members' aggression, derision, and desire to, or need to, destroy the therapists' strength, based on what they saw in their union as a "straight" couple, led them to attempt to emasculate them, to render them an infertile couple. This was mirrored in both therapists, and it escalated to the point of them feeling in a concrete way like an impotent couple unable to do any good or to give effective emotional nurturing. Somnolence and sleepiness was then their way of reacting in a concrete way to patients' envious attacks on them and their denial of accepting any symbolic mental representations. This confusion reached a peak threatening their own gender identity, by producing reciprocal dreams which represented the break-up of their union and a sense of being literally blind, humiliated, and castrated.

As some awareness of the patients' own defences and denial began to take place through the integration of the "other" in the admission of the other gender (that is, female patients who expressed a wish to explore wanting to become males), some socialization and an incipient insight were in evidence.

This unique opportunity gave both therapists a rich learning experience, which could enable them to engage in further research regarding transferential and countertransferential processes in dealing with the many challenges encountered with this patient population. The fact that the group has continued in a healthy way for nine years now, with another therapist, is itself evidence that the initial work was worthwhile, despite, or perhaps because of, the initial enormous difficulties.

## References

Argentieri, S. (2006). Trasvestitismo, transessualismo, transgender. *Psicoanalisi, 10*(2): 78–79.

Benjamin, H. (1953). Transvestism and transsexualism. *International Journal of Sexology, 7*(1):12–14.

Chiland, C. (2005). *Exploring Transsexualism*. London: Karnac.

Greer, G. (1999). *The Whole Woman*. London: Doubleday.

Hakeem, A. (2007). Transsexuality: a case of the emperor's new clothes. In: D. Morgan & S. Ruszczynski (Eds.), *Lectures on Violence Perversion and Delinquency, The Portman Papers* (179–192). London: Karnac.

Hopper, E. (2003). *Traumatic Experience in the Unconscious Life of Groups: The Fourth Basic Assumption-Incohesion—Aggregation/Massification*. London: Jessica Kingsley.

Limentani, A.(1979.) The significance of transsexualism in relation to some basic psychoanalytic concepts. *International Review of Psychoanalysis, 6*: 139–153.

Lothstein, L.M. (1979). Psychodynamics and sociodynamics of gender-dysphoric states. *American Journal of Psychotherapy, 33*: 214–238.

Mitchell, J. (2006a). Using Winnicott to understand gender/social sex. Lecture given at the Donald Winnicott Today International Conference, 9–11 June 2006, UCL London.

Mitchell, J. (2006b). Gender and the environment. Lecture given at the Donald Winnicott Today International Conference 9–11 June 2006, UCL London.

Motz, A. (2008). *The Psychology of Female Violence*. London: Routledge.

Person, E. S. (1994). *The Sexual Century*. New Haven, CT: Yale University Press, 1999.

Stoller, R. (1968). *Sex and Gender* (volume 1). New York: Science House [2nd edn. New York: Jason Aronson, 1974].

Thurer, S. (2005). *The End of Gender: A Psychological Autopsy*. London: Routledge.

Welldon, E. V. (1988). *Mother, Madonna Whore The Idealisation and Denigration of Motherhood*. London: Free Association Books.

Welldon, E. V. (1996). Contrasts in male and female perversions. In: C. Cordess & M. Cox (Eds.), *Forensic Psychotherapy* (pp. 273–289). London: Jessica Kingsley Publishers.

Winnicott, D. W. (1956). Primary maternal preoccupation. In: *Collected Papers: Through Paediatrics to Psychoanalysis*. London: Tavistock Publications, 1958.

# CHAPTER SIX

# Counterpoints

*Jacqueline Amati Mehler*

I t is a great pleasure for me to have been invited to make a contribution to this volume with some comments about the plenary panel and general discussion that I had the privilege to chair in the COWAP meeting on the subject of this book. One of the merits of the COWAP conference that hosted the papers published here, as well as that of previous meetings mentioned by Giovanna Ambrosio in her introduction, is that it focused from a specific psychoanalytic viewpoint on matters that are closely linked with, and in turn have great impact on, society, on mental health legislation, and on ethical issues.

The difficulties that arise when dealing with transvestism, transsexualism, and transgender are in part related to the pressure for concrete solutions when confronted with the request for sex reassignment; solutions that are often embedded in ideological or social reactions rather than based on in-depth clinical experience and conceptual clarity of the particular psychopathology of the individuals concerned . This is rendered more difficult for two main reasons. First, we must reckon with the fact, mentioned in these papers, that patients who come under the umbrella of "trans" organizations rarely search for or choose psychoanalytic help spontaneously. Second, as Simona Argentieri illustrates in her contribution, while transsexuals and transvestites are very different, today, "in the general defensive tendency towards indifferentiation . . . the two famous differences of the Oedipal crossroads, between child and adult and between male and female . . . seem to be less significant for the construction of identity", thus giving rise to what she has called "the grey zone", with blurred boundaries of the different "trans" conditions. (I shall come back to this later.) What risks being underestimated is the conceptual background of such conditions, the differentiation between transvestism and transsexualism, as well as its nosographic place. In this sense, the reader will find an interesting arena for thought on account of the diversity of sources of the material presented, and because of the authors' different personal theories.

The clinical material is derived from direct psychoanalytic and in-depth psychotherapeutic experience with such cases (see Argentieri), as well as from experiences stemming from therapeutic and consultative work with children, adolescents, and with their parents (see Di Ceglie and Chiland), and also from group work with patients who have already undergone bodily transformation (see Welldon) .

The variety of the material discussed is partly the consequence of local legislations establishing a clear-cut pathway that has to be followed by individuals who seek help in order to obtain surgical intervention to change sex, as well as modification of their civil status. Compulsory psychological consultation for a certain period is required so as to ascertain conviction about the wish to change sex and gender identity. What is less explored, however, due to the few cases that come for personal in-depth treatment following bodily mutilations and drastic physical and functional change, is the psychic outcome connected to it that varies according to individual facts for which a statistical outlook falls short. Therefore, Argentieri's attempt to put in place some interesting hypotheses about the different psychic organization underlying the two categories of transsexuals and transvestites, which current trends attempt to assemble under the same "trans" umbrella, is a crucial contribution to this complex matter and the main interest of this volume.

Argentieri describes her personal clinical experience within a psychoanalytic and psychotherapeutic setting, and in a most scholarly way attempts to formulate the ins and outs of the psychic organization and functioning of transvestites and transsexuals. Her discussant, Chiland, offers her vast experience in consultative work with psychologists and doctors dealing with patients who want to have a sex reassignment. She also belongs to a small team of psychoanalysts in France who offer psychoanalytic help (usually psychotherapy treatment) to transsexuals and transvestites. Her experience resembles that of most of us in the sense that rarely do such patients seek psychoanalytic help. Chiland also shares with us her main experience: that of a catamnestic study of patients who had already undergone an operation to change sex.

Chiland and Argentieri share some views and disagree on others. I shall try to focus on some of the issues that allowed for a lively discussion, and highlight unresolved questions that call for further psychoanalytic reflection. The reason for concentrating most of my commentaries on these two contributions is because, while agreements produced a vast platform of consensus among all the contributors, conceptual and clinical controversies that enlivened the discussion derived mainly from the Argentieri–Chiland discussion. The panel by Di Ceglie and Torres de Beà presented us with another meaningful outlook to which I shall refer in more detail below.

The first question raised by Argentieri (about which, surprisingly enough, clarity is anything but straightforward) regards whether the "trans" cases have really increased, or whether mass media has drawn public attention towards a phenomenon that has always existed. She is inclined to think that perhaps current psychosocial circumstances favour what she considers particular defensive organizations, and she raises two main questions.

First, do transsexuals and transvestites conform to the same syndrome and, second, are transsexualism and transvestism to be considered perversions?

Regarding the first point, Argentieri considers them to be very different, and Chiland agrees with her. Transvestites (usually men) who dress up like women have a different psychopathological organization from transsexuals. Transvestites do not change sex, whereas sex reassignment is the characteristic feature of transsexuals. Many readers may consider this distinction superfluous, because it appears to be self-evident. But while this is so from a purely descriptive viewpoint, when the discussion comes down to trying to sort out the psychopathology and its metapsychological background, we are confronted with the constraints imposed on each of us by our own implicit or explicit psychoanalytic paradigms.

While Argentieri differentiates these two syndromes based on the developmental drive organization, Chiland puts more emphasis on what she calls the identity components, such as the transsexual component and the homosexual component. In this regard Di Ceglie refers to some follow-up studies (not many) to ascertain the outcome in adulthood of children and adolescents who show gender identity disorders. Although a significant number of cases develop homosexual or bisexual identities, Di Ceglie remarks that, for the majority of children, "the experience of an atypical gender identity is transient" and that the connection between the child or adolescent gender disorder and a gay identity is not clear.

For Argentieri, transvestites are more evolved and maintain their sexuality manifested through erotization of the transvested body. Individuals such as these, as she shows with clinical material, are men who usually maintain desire for, and enjoy sex with, women. Excitation is highly reinforced, however, if they can make love to women when they themselves are dressed as females. Illusion is maintained, and Argentieri places such functioning in the area of transitional phenomena. In other words, while they play with illusion, they maintain their sexuality.

In the case of transsexuals, this author puts emphasis on the concreteness of the body and the mutilation undergone that, in her mind, sacrifices sexuality and privileges surface sensoriality that prevails over sexuality. Presymbolic levels tend to replace illusion by delusion, "a typical circumscribed delusion". From a metapsychological viewpoint, Argentieri and Chiland have different ideas, but it is interesting to note that both agree on the fact that the idea of "changing one's sex is a mad one, since it is in itself impossible . . . it is only the appearance of that person's body and civil status . . ." that can change. This raises both the relationship to the reality principle in such patients and the issue of the classic defensive combination of disavowal and consequent splitting of the ego that saves a quota of the personality from psychosis. As mentioned above, Chiland considers that an important homosexual component is present, and she thinks that perhaps some transsexuals were initially transvestites. In some way, this might seem to contradict her full agreement with Argentieri about transsexuals and transvestites being very different. On the other hand, it opens up the complex chapter of the so-called *grey zone* that compels us to think about what contemporary psychoanalysis can contribute to our formulation of early psychic organization and its place within classical metapsychological considerations.

Argentieri believes that these organizations fall into the realm of perversions, whereas Chiland, although she agrees that we are confronted with perversions, disagrees with Argentieri when she says that transsexuals elude the level of drives. In fact, from a classical viewpoint, it would be difficult to consider a perversion devoid of sexuality.

Here, two crucial questions arise. First, what kind of *sexuality* are we talking about? We should recall Freud's important statement in Chapter III of *An Outline of Psycho-Analysis* (1940a, p. 152): "It is necessary to distinguish sharply between the concepts of sexual and genital". Argentieri focuses on the importance of early pre-Oedipal vicissitudes that are subsequently retroactively resignified at the time of the Oedipal crossroad, which is when the perversion is organized. Chiland also quotes Freud, who "in his discussion of neurosis pointed out that there were more mixed cases than pure ones". But are we in the realm of neurosis? While this may be pertinent for some cases belonging to the so-called grey zone, Argentieri, as I have said, definitely places transvestism and transsexualism among the perversions.

This brings us to the second question. What do we mean by perversions? As I had occasion to mention in a paper presented at the 1995 IPA Congress in San Francisco (Amati Mehler, 1999), besides being confronted with a kaleidoscopic outlook on perversions—according to the different theoretical models—today, many analysts have extended the term to such a broad spectrum as to encompass any action, or the utilization of things, with an aim that is at variance with the one usually proposed. Culture, morals, and ideology, rather than metapsychological considerations, also tend to condition definitions and discussion about what was originally coined in psychoanalysis as perverse psycho-sexual organizations.

At that time, the aim of my reflections was restricted to an attempt to make a distinction between perversions understood as a structural organization or a syndrome, and perversions as perverse features: that is, a series of phenomena that, to my mind, respond to perverse symptoms or mechanisms not related to the specific psychic structure as described by Freud. Two core issues are related to the classical description of perversions as mentioned above: one deals with the defence mechanisms (disavowal and splitting) that Argentieri, as well as the other contributors, agreed upon as being distinctive in the case of transsexuals. The other issue regards those anxieties that, under the general heading of castration anxiety, differ according to the different developmental levels to which they belong.[1]

Thus, when referring to perversions today, several questions come to mind, and I believe that if we do not take these into account, discussions about whether transsexualism and transvestism (as Argentieri believes and I personally agree) are or are not perversions becomes very difficult. Some of these questions regard: (a) whether we are still referring to *sexual perversions*, as described by Freud; that is, to a deviant sexuality as far as the aim or the object of the libidinal drives are concerned; (b) whether this implies a specific psychopathological *structure*, related to the concept of *Spaltung* (ego split) caused by the mechanism of *disavowal* aimed at denying the perception of castration; (c) or whether we mean *symptoms*, or other multiform phenomena, such as perverse defences, perverse phantasies, or perverse behaviour in character disorders, perverse thought processes, a perverse transference (Reed, 1994, p. 164), or simple perversity in the sense of wickedness.

Therefore, whenever the word "perversion" is used, it requires a conceptual and a clinical re-definition.[2]

As far as the first point (a) is concerned, some of Argentieri's interesting formulations explore precisely whether perversions are mainly connected to the vicissitudes of pre-genital libidinal or aggressive drive components (related to the Freudian polymorph perverse phase) along their path to the solution of the Oedipal complex; or whether there is a "pre-history" of perversions, which implies that we should broaden our thinking so as to include other areas of psychic functioning, that is, those that *precede* structural organization. The problems posed are not only clinical, but also metapsychological and require a better definition of what we mean by "sexual". This calls for Freud's recommendation that, when referring to "sexual", it would be more appropriate to refer to "psychosexuality". The latter implies the complexity of the developmental drive vicissitudes and their access to representation, and the evolution of partial sexual components on their way to integration and genitality, from narcissism to object relations. Thus, we need to consider, on one hand, early mental mechanisms related to annihilation anxieties within a scenario of self-object undifferentiation, and, on the other hand, the use of defence mechanisms such as disavowal (point c) which cause more or less permanent structural changes in the ego.

In his *Outline of Psycho-Analysis* (1940a) Freud extends the idea of ego splitting—as a result of disavowal—beyond cases of fetishism and psychosis and into neurosis in general, which is particularly relevant to our discussion about perversions and psychic (internal) reality. But what counts most in Freud's description is that the *Spaltung* continues to be a consequence of two contrary tendencies that, in cases of perversion and psychosis, find themselves coexisting intrasystematically, that is, inside of the ego; whereas in neurosis one of these tendencies belongs to the ego and the other to the id. The difference between the cases of neurosis and those of fetishism and of psychosis would thus be essentially topographical, or structural.

On the one hand, the classical Freudian definition of perversion requires the presence of sexual pleasure within the perverse act. On the other, a better knowledge of early psychic scenarios takes into account a more archaic form of psychosensorial excitation in search of appeasement that should be differentiated from sexual genital excitement. Excitation seems to be connected essentially with the search for contact and fusional experiences (detached from genital satisfaction), or in quest of what Freud called the specific binding action from the environment lest the barrier of stimuli be defeated. All this raises the issue of agreement and/or disagreement about different stages of sexuality, and different opinions about what is sexual. In fact, whereas Argentieri considers that transsexuals sacrifice genital sexuality in the sense that they are the expression of a pathological outcome of the oedipal sexual organization, Chiland, as I will illustrate below, disagrees with this.

The way we use the concept of splitting might account for one of the possible bedrocks of theoretical controversy that require conceptual bridges. Contrary to the pathological splitting of the fetishist that merely increases with time, we can observe more mobile and mutant splittings that decompose and recompose changing figures (Amati Mehler, 1999). Mechanisms such as these account for the grey zone of ambiguous situations that, in accordance with Argentieri, I would number among those situations that come close to what I defined in the paper mentioned above as perverse behaviour, symptoms. or defence mechanisms; whereas "the Freudian ego Splitting invoked to explain perversions is a consequence of the defensive process and not a defence mechanism itself" (Amati Mehler, Argentieri, & Canestri, 1993). Splitting could be a structural or a dynamic concept according to the models used. Argentieri mentions "micro-splittings or regressions to ambiguity" that characterize such perverse behaviours "at the elusive limit between normality and pathology", such as "sex tourism", addiction to pornographic films, or the occasional or systematic visiting of paedophilic Internet sites by "normal nice boys and fathers of families . . . facilitated by the unemotional de-responsibility due to the remote and anonymous quality of the material in question".

What some authors describe as perverse mechanisms—for example, perverse thought processes or perverse transference—could thus be related to more mobile and dynamic (splitting or other) processes, whereas what other authors refer to as sexual perversions concern a particular psychic structural organization, ensuing in the compulsion to repeat a pattern of specific and ritual ceremonials in order to reach orgiastic pleasure. Although, as Argentieri points out, we might encounter combined situations, she tends to situate transsexuals and transvestites in the realm of perversions in which a circumscribed delusion prevails over the rest of the functioning ego, which brings us back to the problem of the link between perversions and psychic reality, a core issue in the case of transsexuals. Space does not allow me to expand on Bleger's (1973) theories, appropriately invoked by Argentieri, about a "symbiotic nucleus", an isolated archaic depository that, because it is isolated and split off, allows the rest of the ego to function in contact with reality.

Thus, while sexuality and castration still play a crucial role in modern contributions on perversions, we are confronted with different possible models depending on how we envision the fate of sexuality in relation to the vicissitudes of primary narcissism and undifferentiated stages of development. The latter envisage pre-structural, non-drive-conflictual stages of development that have particularly drawn Argentieri's attention, whereas the identity issues also deeply enmeshed with these syndromes seemed to be the most salient aspects for Chiland. Although Argentieri insists on early features of psychic organization related to narcissistic and self- or hetero-directed destructiveness, she emphasizes that the Oedipus crux remains the organizing or disorganizing core of perverse pathology. What she emphasizes is the need to explore how the two levels—pre-Oedipal and Oedipal—are imbricated with each other.

Actually, there is no real disagreement on this, except perhaps that Argentieri puts emphasis on the role of primary identifications involving non-differentiation and imitation as a precursor of real identifications. She also focuses on the early bodily aspects and phantasies *about* the body as distinct from phantasies *in* the body, as formulated by Gaddini (1982).

But let me further focus on the main disgreements between Argentieri and Chiland. Although they both agree that in trans-sexuals denial and splitting prevail, Chiland thinks that not all transsexuals have psychotic traits, nor does she place them all among perversions. Of course, this again touches upon the *grey zone*, but, in my opinion, it raises the question of something else as well. Contemporary psychoanalysis has led many analysts to consider that different levels of psychic functioning can coexist, and even predominant neurotic organizations can host psychotic nuclei. I believe that the main discrepancies between Argentieri and Chiland do not regard the descriptive aspects, nor do they disagree about the existence in transsexuals of "a typical circumscribed delusion"; but, to the metapsychological queries that come up, the two authors give a different response.

For example, Chiland does not believe, as Argentieri does, that men and women present the same psychopathology from a metapsychological viewpoint. Chiland writes that babies experience emotions with their bodies, and therefore differently according to whether they are boys or girls; while they are babies, they do not realize whether they are "boys" or "girls", but greater muscular tonicity and penile erections are present in boys, while girls have a more diffuse experience of their bodies. Whereas I agree that anatomy influences destiny, and although I might differ in this from Argentieri, it does not prevent me from agreeing with her that the psychopathological organization is the same in male and female transsexuals, precisely because of what Chiland herself mentions above: that, at early stages, "while babies are babies they do not realize whether they are boys or girls".

Chiland also does not accept Argentieri's claim what while transvestites preserve their sexual gender identity and the use of drives, accompanied by intense erotization of the transvested body, transsexuals, through mutilation of the parts of the body that represent it, sacrifice sexuality. Both issues are related because on one hand they regard the concept itself of sexuality, and on the other hand they regard the question of whether we can identify aggressiveness as a male component and passivity as a female feature, as Chiland believes. As already mentioned, in Ambrosio's Introduction she is inclined to think that rejection of maleness is connected with rejection of aggressiveness[3] altogether, and rejection of femaleness is equated with rejection of passivity. Argentieri, instead, considers that, contrary to classical views that assign perversion and aggressiveness only to men, transsexualism is the proof that women also can be perverts, as Welldon has shown in her seminal book *Mother, Madonna, Whore*. For Argentieri, passiveness and activity-aggressiveness are not characteristic of male or female. Chiland, instead, claims that

> rejecting maleness is the refusal of activity that is inevitably likened to aggressiveness, which leads this author to consider that refusing maleness and refusing femaleness are not of the same nature as far as the structure of the mind is concerned.

While this may be true from a descriptive viewpoint, as Chiland learnt from her clinical experience, perhaps we should distinguish thoughts that have a sociological or cultural imprint from what is a structural psychic organization.

Here there is a real gap between Argentieri's and Chiland's paradigms. Argentieri refers to a period (involved in transsexualism) regarding a developmental stage in which the corporeal perceptions of male–female diversity at such early stages of development are not to be identified as gender identity, although it does constitute the starting point of its destiny as it develops within the specific quality of the child–parent relationship with its multi-faceted drive and socio-cultural vicissitudes. For Chiland, identity is always sexual, since she rejects the above-mentioned undifferentiated stage of development. She says, "Identity is at first in the parent's mind", which, although true, might not solve the above discrepancies. The latter elements would also be in the background of what becomes the variable about the evaluation of analysability in each patient and/or, as I shall mention below, to the experience that Di Ceglie has brought to our attention in his work with children.

Chiland thinks that transsesxuals are sexually attracted by people of the same sex (and here, of course, the complex issue of homosexuality comes into play again), whereas Argentieri believes that transsexuals essentially give up drives, whether hetero or homosexual. To this, Chiland replies by quoting from her consulting experience with a man-to-woman transsexual, who stated, "I have a woman's orgasm." It is less clear, however, what a person might understand a "woman's orgasm" to be, and how sexuality is subjectivated. Welldon remarks that, in previous times, therapists associated homosexuality with the psychopathology of patients who felt trapped in the body of a person with a different gender. Following Stoller and her own experience, she focuses more on the projection of the internal conflict about gender. She quotes cases in which a panic attack follows the facilitating acceptance by the doctor of their request for change, and the urge to consult another doctor in the hope of finding an opposite position.

Based on her consulting experience, Chiland is less pessimistic than Argentieri about the post-surgical effect on transsexuals, and from her consulting work she sees an overall less pessimistic outcome. Perhaps this depends on the fact that Argentieri's experience, as described in her presentation, regards patients in whom the illusion of being well if only a sexual change can be obtained, is defeated by the failure of the illusion and the distress and suffering that it entails *a posteriori*.

In the opening remarks of her presentation, Welldon remarks that transsexualism is a complex and delicate situation that ". . . can briefly be descibed as a self-diagnosis followed by a self-prescibed cure". This self-conviction is sustained with unrelenting rigidity, and when professionally dealt with and confronted with the "irrational" requests of the patients, produces a sense of confusion. In this she agrees with Chiland, who claims that "to such mad requests doctors have responded with mad offers". Welldon lucidly shares with us her therapeutic experience with groups of men and women with gender disorders, and also with patients on their way to requesting a sexual reassignment. She organized these groups in an attempt to get a better understanding from a psychodynamic perspective, while at the same time alert to Stoller's remark that the general rule applied to transsexuals is that whatever is done—even nothing—will show itself to be wrong. What I regard as meaningful is Welldon's straightforward admission of the sense of humiliation and emotional wound that she and her colleagues felt as a result of their work. They had hoped, using Chiland's words, to "explore with the patient who or what he or she is and leave as many doors open as possible".

As the reader will see, in Welldon's chapter the clinical vignettes described give a vivid picture of the emotionally charged interaction between the therapist, the co-therapist, and the patients.

Let me refer now to Di Ceglie's experience, because he shares with us the exploration and assessment of early manifestations of gender disorders, their individual meaning, and the possible management of such conditions.

This author introduces his paper by quoting from Homer's *Odyssey* the passage describing the danger Ulysses is confronted with when passing between the two dangerous "cliffs", Scylla and Charybdis. His aim is to provide a meaningful metaphor for the danger to privilege in such cases either body or the mind, whereas the problem lies in "falling foul of either of these two polarities". Di Ceglie's views differ from those of Stoller, who refers to the concept of "core gender identity" as being fully developed before the phallic stage, although it continues to develop even beyond adolescence. Stoller also claims that the beliefs comprising the "mental structure" of the core gender identity are the earliest part of gender identity and are relatively permanent after age 4–5. Chiland would probably agree with this. Di Ceglie claims that his own experience leads him to think that, in some children, there may be more flexibility in gender identity than that formulated by Stoller. In fact, Di Ceglie and Freedman (1998) has included under the umbrella concept of "atypical gender identity organization" (AGIO) as a specific clinical entity encompassing cases that differ according to criteria of rigidity *vs.* flexibility, cases that vary according to the developmental stage at which the atypical organization occurs and also according to the kind of trauma experienced in childhood.

Although Di Ceglie admits that biological factors might contribute to AGIO, and although he quotes that certain specific brain findings have been described in some transsexuals, these data are uncertain and, in his opinion, whether they might contribute to AGIO is not really known.

Torres de Beà, who was Di Ceglie's discussant, seems to be more inclined than he is to consider the impact on the workings of the mind of biological or even genetic factors in gender identity disorders. She dedicates much attention in her paper to early interactions of mother–foetus in the womb as possibly influencing every aspect of evolution, and, while she admits that not much is validated, she makes an appeal not to disregard such issues. Although she mentions psychological or socio-cultural facts in the development of personal identities in general, Torres de Beà calls our attention to the fact that these are more or less "visible" or conscious facts, whereas phantasies and cross-gender identity projections are more difficult to detect. In this sense, the clinical presentations of Di Ceglie show in the dialogue with the child called Max, and the work with the parents how some of these factors can be explored and be helpful in guiding the therapist's possible or impossible task. Torres de Beà, like Chiland, focuses on issues that regard the processes of identification. The case of Jane, mentioned by Di Ceglie, is quite significant in this sense. Identifications, though, bring up the problem of which kinds of identifications we refer to, whether primary or secondary. The case of Jane refers to very early processes of identification with the lost attachment object, and the outcome of her therapy, started at an early age, was rather rewarding in dealing with her core gender identity disorder. Torres de Beà wonders about problems of countertransference in working with such cases, and though Di Ceglie does not use this term, he speaks about prejudice and how this can lead therapists to being, as he calls them, "crusaders" for one or other solution rather than trying to help children and parents explore and understand the underlying psychological facts involved in the painful dramas that reveal themselves in consultation and treatment.

I cannot close without mentioning again a concern about the social side of matters, which I have expressed elsewhere (1994), in relation to the impact on the fate of gender and general identity of the contemporary socio-cultural tendency towards sexual undifferentiation. Natural frontiers of gender and generation are also currently overcome by scientific practices. Just think of the case of the woman simultaneously the "grandmother" and the biological mother of a baby born through her insemination by the husband of her infertile daughter. There is, I think, a confusion between the social, the ideological, and the psychological levels, between mother and father figures, between male and female and maternal and paternal functions. Unisex and undifferentiation is confused with equality, and seems to have done away with the urge to discover, recognize, and bear the different other, male or female; fused group ties seem to reign over a lost sense of individuality. The significance of undifferentiation as a fertile ground for partial drive components, associated to increased violence (in its turn amplified by mass media), accounts for what some authors have identified as a socio-cultural scenario that suggests, as our contributors have highlighted, disquieting affinities with perverse relational strategies that challenge our psychoanalytic tools.

## Notes

1.    In 1923, Freud added to the case on Little Hans (1909b) the following footnote on the castration complex as further developed in contributions to the subject by Lou Andreas-Salome:

> It has been urged that every time his mother's breast is withdrawn from a baby he is bound to feel it as castration (that is to say, as the loss of what he regards as an important part of his own body); that, further, he cannot fail to be similarly affected by the regular loss of his faeces; and, finally, that the act of birth itself (consisting as it does in the separation of the child from his mother with whom he has hitherto been united) is the prototype of all castration . . .

2.  Although Laplanche and Pontalis (1973) write in the *Vocabulary of Psychoanalysis* that "in psychoanalysis the word perversion is used exclusively in relation to sexuality", some authors (e.g., Cooper in his paper on "The unconscious core of perversion" [1991]) remind us that many analysts would today consider "aspects of aggressive and narcissistic activities as the major source of behaviours we would label perverse" (p. 19).

3.  One could, of course, also wonder whether, in males who reject maleness, the sex reassignment is not also connected with the envy of what are perceived as omnipotent mothers, who have breasts and can have babies.

## References

Amati Mehler, J. (1994). Further considerations on love, impotence and male sexuality. *Canadian Journal of Psychoanalysis, 2*: 135–150.

Amati Mehler, J. (1999). Perversioni: struttura, sintomo o meccanismo? *Psicoanalisi, 3*(1): 59–67.

Amati Mehler, J., Argentieri, S., & Canestri, J. (1993). *The Babel of the Unconscious: Mothertongue and Foreign Languages in the Psychoanalytic Dimension.* Madison, CT: International Universities Press.

Bleger, J. (1973). Perversiones. *Revista de Psicoanalisis, XXX*(2).

Cooper, A. (1991). The unconscious core of perversion. In: G. I. Fogel & W. A. Myers (Eds.), *Perversions and Near-Perversions in Clinical Practice.* New Haven, CT: Yale University Press.

Di Ceglie, D., & Freedman, D. (Eds.) (1998). *A Stranger in My Own Body: Atypical Gender Identity Development and Mental Health.* London: Karnac.

Freud, S. (1909b). The analysis of a phobia in a five-year-old boy. *S.E., 10*: 3–149. London: Hogarth.

Freud, S. (1940a). *An Outline of Psycho-Analysis. S.E., 23*: 141–207. London: Hogarth.

Gaddini, E. (1982). Early defensive fantasies and the psychoanalytical process. *International Journal of Psycho-Analysis, 63*: 379–386.

Laplanche, J., & Pontalis, J.-B. (1973). *The Language of Psychoanalysis.* London: Hogarth Press [reprinted London: Karnac, 1988].

Reed, G. (1994). *Transference Neurosis and Psychoanalytic Experience: Perspectives on Contemporary Clinical Practice.* New Haven, CT: Yale University Press.

# INDEX